Interactive Math Notebook: Grade 8

Authors: Schyrlet Cameron and Carolyn Craig
Editor: Mary Dieterich
Proofreaders: Alexis Fey and Margaret Brown

COPYRIGHT © 2020 Mark Twain Media, Inc.

ISBN 978-1-62223-815-6

Printing No. CD-405047

Mark Twain Media, Inc., Publishers
Distributed by Carson-Dellosa Publishing LLC

The purchase of this book entitles the buyer to reproduce the student pages for classroom use only. Other permissions may be obtained by writing Mark Twain Media, Inc., Publishers.

All rights reserved. Printed in the United States of America.

Visit us at www.carsondellosa.com

Table of Contents

To the Teacher

Introduction 1
Organizing an Interactive Notebook 2
Left-hand and Right-hand Notebook Page 3
Interactive Notebook Grading Rubric 3

Unit One: The Number System

    Number Systems 4
    Converting Repeating Decimals to
        Fractions 6
    Estimating Square Roots 8
    Properties of Integer Exponents 10
    Square Roots & Cube Roots 12
    Scientific Notation 14
    Adding & Subtracting With Scientific
        Notation 16
    Multiplying & Dividing With Scientific
        Notation 18

Unit Two: Expressions & Equations

    Solving Multi-Step Equations 20
    Solutions of One-Variable Equations 22
    Solving Systems of Equations
        Graphically 24
    Solving Systems of Equations
        Algebraically 26

Unit Three: Ratios & Proportional Relationships

    Graphing Proportional Relationships 28
    Slope of a Line 30
    Similar Triangles & Slope 32
    Functions 34
    Rate of Change 36
    Linear & Nonlinear Functions 38

Unit Four: Geometry

    Translations on the Coordinate Plane 40
    Reflections on the Coordinate Plane 42
    Rotations on the Coordinate Plane 44
    Dilations on the Coordinate Plane 46
    Angles of Triangles 48
    Pythagorean Theorem 50
    Distance on a Coordinate Plane 52
    Volume of Cones, Cylinders, &
        Spheres 54

Unit 5: Statistics & Probability

    Scatter Plots 56
    Two-Way Tables 58

Answer Keys 60

Introduction

The *Interactive Math Notebook: Grade 8* is designed to allow students to become active participants in their own learning. The book lays out an easy-to-follow plan for setting up, creating, and maintaining an interactive notebook.

An interactive notebook is simply a spiral notebook that students use to store and organize important information. It is a culmination of student work throughout the unit of study. Once completed, the notebook becomes the student's own personalized notebook and a great resource for reviewing and studying for tests.

The intent of the book is to help students make sense of new information. Textbooks often present more facts and data than students can process at one time. This book introduces each concept in an easy-to-read and easy-to-understand format that does not overwhelm the learner. The text presents only the most important information, making it easier for students to comprehend. Vocabulary words are printed in boldfaced type.

The book focuses on the critical areas for mathematics in grade eight. The 28 lessons cover 5 units of study: Number Systems, Expressions and Equations, Ratios and Proportional Relationships, Geometry, and Statistics and Probability. The units can be used in the order presented or in an order that best fits the classroom curriculum. Teachers can easily differentiate units to address the individual learning levels and needs of students. The lessons are designed to support state and national standards. Each lesson consists of two pages that are used to create the right-hand and left-hand pages of the interactive notebook.

- **Input page:** essential information for understanding the lesson concepts and directions for creating the interactive page.
- **Output page:** hands-on activity such as a foldable or graphic organizer to help students process essential information from the lesson.

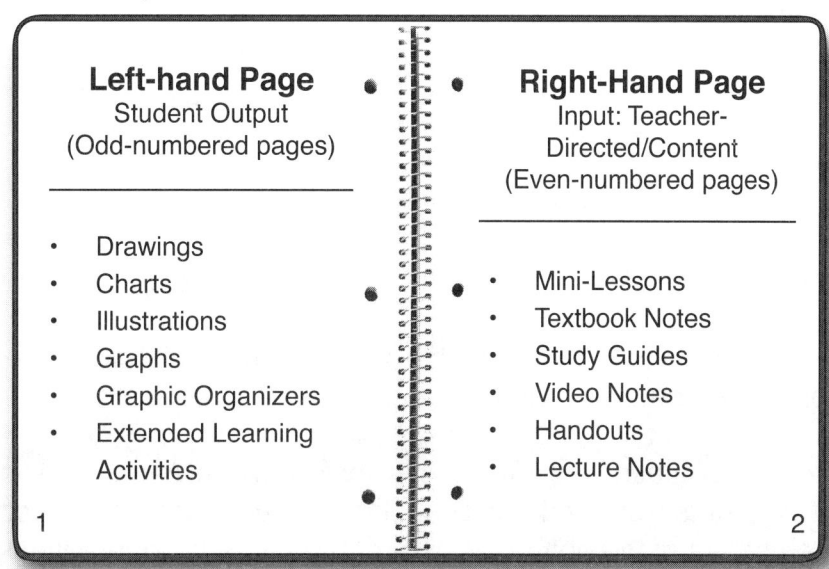

Organizing an Interactive Notebook

What Is an Interactive Notebook?

Does this sound familiar? "I can't find my homework…class notes…study guide." If so, the interactive notebook is a tool you can use to help manage this problem. An interactive notebook is simply a notebook that students use to record, store, and organize their work. The "interactive" aspect of the notebook comes from the fact that students are working with information in various ways as they fill in the notebook. Once completed, the notebook becomes the student's own personalized study guide and a great resource for reviewing information, reinforcing concepts, and studying for tests.

Materials Needed to Create an Interactive Notebook

- Notebook (spiral, composition, or binder with loose-leaf paper)
- Glue stick
- Scissors
- Colored pencils (we do not recommend using markers)
- Tabs

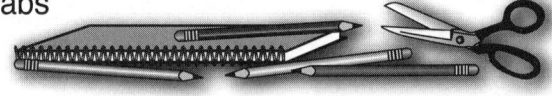

Creating an Interactive Notebook

A good time to introduce the interactive notebook is at the beginning of a new unit of study. Use the following steps to get started.

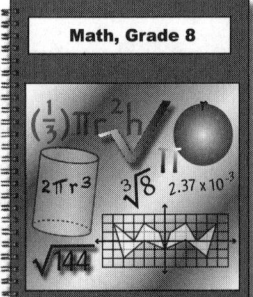

Step 1: *Notebook Cover*
Students design a cover to reflect the units of study. They should add their names and other important information as directed by the teacher.

Step 2: *Grading Rubric*
Take time to discuss the grading rubric with the students. It is important for each student to understand the expectations for creating the interactive notebook.

Step 3: *Table of Contents*
Students label the first several pages of the notebook "Table of Contents." When completing a new page, they add its title to the table of contents.

Step 4: *Creating Pages*
The notebook is developed using the dual-page format. The right-hand side is the input page where essential information and notes from readings, lectures, or videos are placed. The left-hand side is the output page reserved for foldable activities, charts, graphic organizers, etc. Students number the front and back of each page in the bottom outside corner (odd: LEFT-side; even: RIGHT-side).

Step 5: *Tab Units*
Add a tab to the edge of the first page of each unit to make it easy to flip to the unit.

Step 6: *Glossary*
Students reserve several pages at the back of the notebook where they can create a glossary of domain-specific terms encountered in each lesson.

Step 7: *Pocket*
Students need to attach a pocket to the inside of the back cover of the notebook for storage of handouts, returned quizzes, class syllabus, and other items that don't seem to belong on pages of the notebook. This can be an envelope, resealable plastic bag, or students can design their own pocket.

Left-hand and Right-hand Notebook Pages

Interactive notebooks are usually viewed open like a textbook. This allows the student to view the left-hand page and right-hand page at the same time. Teachers have several options for how to format the two pages. Traditionally, the right-hand page is used as the input or the content part of the lesson. The left-hand page is the student output part of the lesson. This is where the students have an opportunity to show what they have learned in a creative and colorful way. (Color helps the brain remember information.)

The format of the interactive notebook involves both the right-brain and left-brain hemispheres to help students process information. When creating the pages, start with the left-hand page. First, have students date the page. Students then move to the right-hand page and the teacher-directed part of the lesson. Finally, students use the information they have learned to complete the left-hand page. Above is an example of completed right- and left-hand pages.

Left-hand Page   **Right-Hand Page**

Interactive Notebook Grading Rubric

Interactive Math Notebook: Grade 8, Grading Rubric				
Category	**4**	**3**	**2**	**1**
Table of Contents	Table of contents is complete.	Table of contents is mostly complete.	Table of contents is somewhat complete.	Attempt was made to include table of contents.
Organization	All pages in correct order. All are numbered, dated, and titled correctly.	Most pages in correct order. Most are numbered, dated, and titled correctly.	Some pages in correct order. Some are numbered, dated, and titled correctly.	Few pages in correct order. Few are numbered, dated, and titled correctly.
Content	All information complete, accurate, and placed in the correct order. All spelling correct.	Most information complete, accurate, and placed in the correct order. Most spelling correct.	Some information complete, accurate, and placed in the correct order. Some spelling errors.	Few pages correctly completed. Many spelling errors.
Appearance	All notebook pages are neat and colorful.	Most notebook pages are neat and colorful.	Some notebook pages are neat and colorful.	Few notebook pages are neat and colorful.
Teacher's Comments:				

Interactive Math Notebook: Grade 8   Student Instructions: Number Systems

Student Instructions: Number Systems

Read the following information. Cut out the mini-lesson and attach it to the right-hand page of your interactive notebook. Use what you have learned to create the left-hand page.

Mini-Lesson

Number Systems

Real numbers are a combination of all the number systems. Examples of real numbers could be any number. There are five categories within the set of real numbers.

Real Numbers
Combination of all the number systems

Includes these categories

Rational Numbers
Can be expressed as the ratio of two whole numbers; includes all integers, fractions, repeating and terminating decimals
$\{-3, 9, 0.75, \frac{1}{2}\}$

Integers
Natural numbers, their opposites or negative numbers, and zero
$\{\ldots -3, -2, -1, 0, 1, 2, 3, \ldots\}$

Whole Numbers
Natural numbers plus zero
$\{0, 1, 2, 3, 4, \ldots\}$

Natural Numbers
Sometimes called counting numbers
$\{1, 2, 3, 4, \ldots\}$

Irrational Numbers
Cannot be expressed as a ratio
$\sqrt{2}$, Pi (π) = 3.14159...
(decimal goes on forever with no pattern)

Some numbers belong to more than one category.

Number	Rational	Integer	Whole	Natural
21	x	x	x	x
-5	x	x		

A real number is a number that can be found on the number line.

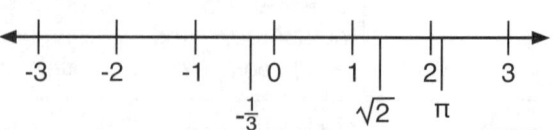

Create Your Left-hand Notebook Page
Step 1: Cut out the title and glue it to the top of the notebook page.
Step 2: Cut out the *What's the Difference?* flap book. Apply glue to the back of the gray center section. Attach it below the title. Under each flap, write the definition.
Step 3: Fill in the *Categorizing Real Numbers* chart. Cut out the chart. Apply glue to the back and attach it below the title.
Step 4: Cut out the *Real Numbers* flap book. Under each flap, write the definition.

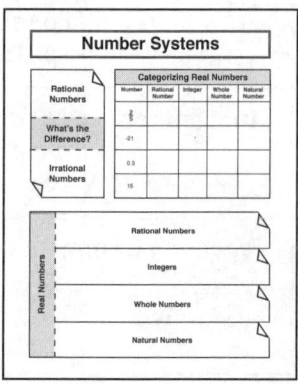

CD-405047 © Mark Twain Media, Inc., Publishers

Number Systems

Rational Numbers

What's the Difference?

Irrational Numbers

Categorizing Real Numbers

Number	Rational Number	Integer	Whole Number	Natural Number
$\frac{2}{6}$				
-21				
0.3				
15				

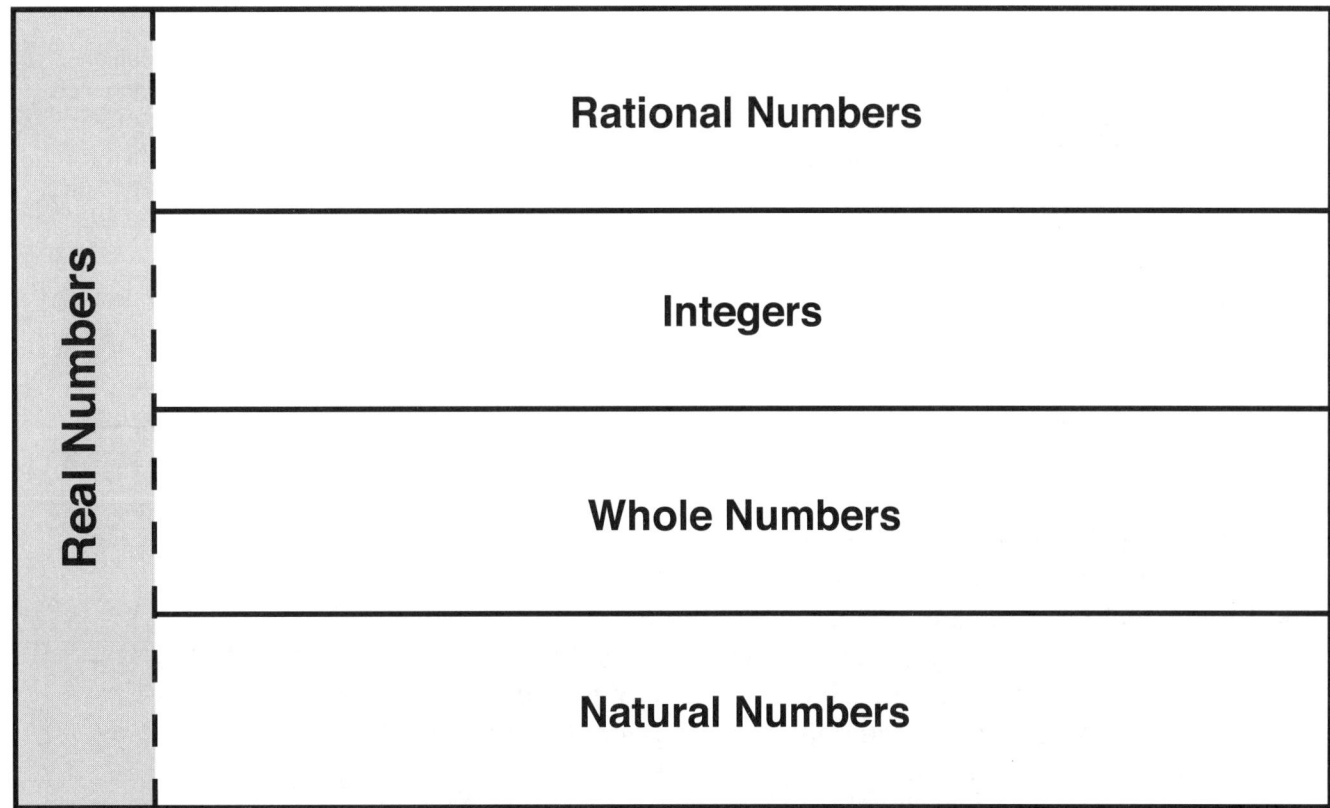

Real Numbers
- Rational Numbers
- Integers
- Whole Numbers
- Natural Numbers

Interactive Math Notebook: Grade 8 — Student Instructions: Converting Repeating Decimals to Fractions

Student Instructions: Converting Repeating Decimals to Fractions

Read the following information. Cut out the mini-lesson and attach it to the right-hand page of your interactive notebook. Use what you have learned to create the left-hand page.

Mini-Lesson

Converting Repeating Decimals to Fractions

All rational numbers (that is, a fraction in simplest form) can be written as either a **terminating decimal** or a **repeating decimal**.

Steps to Convert a Fraction to a Decimal
Step 1: Divide the numerator of the fraction by the denominator.
Step 2: Determine if the answer is a terminating or repeating decimal.
 • When the remainder is zero, it is called a **terminating decimal**.
 • If the remainder begins to repeat, it is called a **repeating decimal**. A bar notation (¯) is used to show that a digit or group of digits repeats. The bar is only placed above the digit or digits that are repeated.

Fraction	Decimal	Type of Decimal
$\frac{1}{3}$	$0.333\ldots = 0.\overline{3}$	repeating decimal
$\frac{1}{2}$	$0.5000 = 0.5$	terminating decimal
$\frac{2}{11}$	$0.1818\ldots = 0.\overline{18}$	repeating decimal

Steps to Convert a Repeating Decimal to a Fraction
 Example: Write $0.\overline{5}$ as a simplified fraction.
Step 1: Let a variable be equal to the repeating decimal you are trying to convert to a fraction. ⟶ $x = 0.5555\ldots$
Step 2: Multiply the variable by the correct power of 10. (If 1 digit repeats, multiply by 10; 2 digits repeat, multiply by 100; 3 digits, multiply by 1,000.) ⟶ $10x = 10(0.5555)$ [Multiply each side by 10 because one digit repeats.]
$10x = 5.555$
Step 3: Subtract the original values from each side to remove the repeating part of the decimal. ⟶ $-x = 0.5555$
$9x = 5$
Step 4: Solve for the variable. ⟶ $x = \frac{5}{9}$ [Simplify by dividing each side by 9.]

Create Your Left-hand Notebook Page

Step 1: Cut out the title and glue it to the top of the notebook page.
Step 2: Complete the *Fraction to Decimal* table. Cut out the piece. Apply glue to the back and attach it below the title.
Step 3: Complete the problem on the front of the *Repeating Decimal to Fraction* flap book. Cut out the book. Cut on the solid lines to create four flaps. Apply glue to the back of the right-hand section and attach it at the bottom of the page. Under each flap, describe the step.

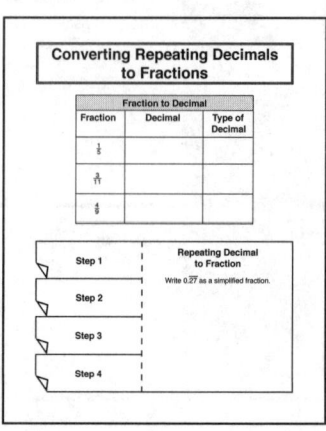

CD-405047 © Mark Twain Media, Inc., Publishers

Converting Repeating Decimals to Fractions

Fraction to Decimal		
Fraction	**Decimal**	**Type of Decimal**
$\frac{1}{5}$		
$\frac{3}{11}$		
$\frac{4}{9}$		

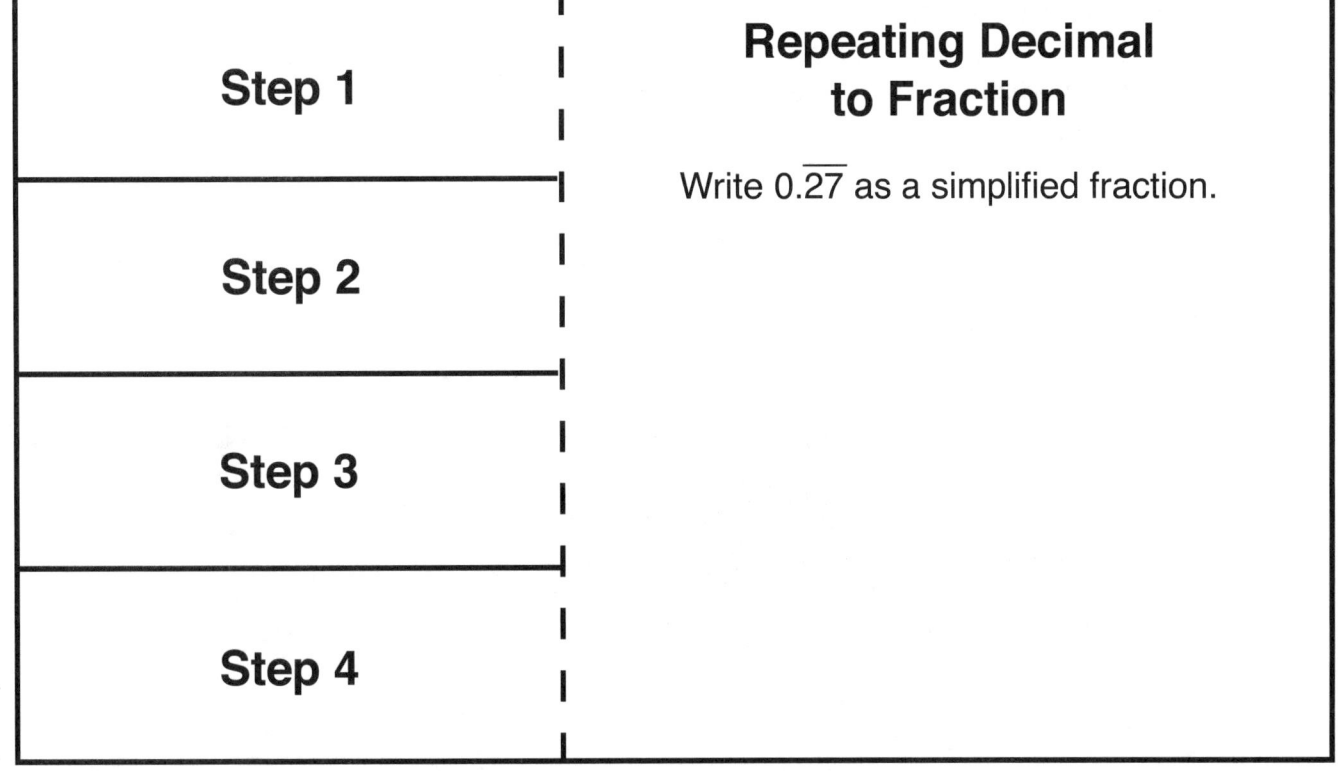

Step 1

Step 2

Step 3

Step 4

Repeating Decimal to Fraction

Write $0.\overline{27}$ as a simplified fraction.

Interactive Math Notebook: Grade 8 — Student Instructions: Estimating Square Roots

Student Instructions: Estimating Square Roots

Read the following information. Cut out the mini-lesson and attach it to the right-hand page of your interactive notebook. Use what you have learned to create the left-hand page.

Mini-Lesson

Estimating Square Roots

The **square** of a number is the number times itself. For example, the square of 6 or 6^2 is $6 \cdot 6 = 36$.
The **square root** is the number that when multiplied times itself equals the square. For example, 6 is a square root of 36.

A **radical sign**, $\sqrt{}$ is used to show the positive square root. The given number inside the radical sign is called the **radicand**.

the square root of 36 → $\boxed{6} \cdot 6 = \boxed{36}$ ← the square of 6

radical sign → $\sqrt{36}$ ← radicand

Perfect squares are numbers that have a square root that is an integer. It is important to recognize perfect squares. The first ten perfect square numbers are: 1, 4, 9, 16, 25, 36, 49, 64, 81, and 100. The square root of a **non-perfect square** is not an integer. The symbol ≈ means "is approximately" and is used because the number has been rounded off to provide an estimate of the exact root value.

Steps to Estimating Square Roots

Example: Estimate $\sqrt{21}$ to the nearest hundredth.

Step 1: Pick the two perfect squares that are just below and above the number you are looking for. → The square root of 16 = **4**; the square root of 25 = **5**. So, the square root of 21 is between the whole numbers 4 and 5.

Step 2: Find the difference between the radicand and the lower perfect square, and find the difference between the two perfect squares. → $21 - 16 = 5$
$25 - 16 = 9$

Step 3: Write the difference as a ratio. Divide to rewrite the fraction as a decimal. → $\frac{5}{9}$ $5 \div 9 \approx 0.56$

Step 4: Combine the smaller whole number square root found in Step 1 and the decimal part for an estimate of the square root. → $(4 + 0.56 = 4.56)$
So, $\sqrt{21}$ is ≈ **4.56**

Create Your Left-hand Notebook Page

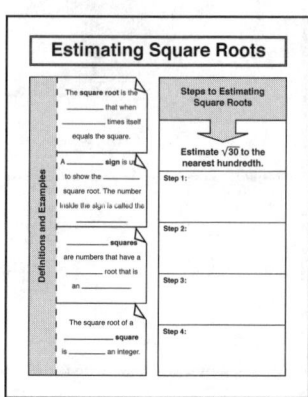

Step 1: Cut out the title and glue it to the top of the notebook page.
Step 2: Fill in the blanks on the *Definitions and Examples* flap book. Cut out the flap book. Apply glue to the back of the gray tab and attach it below the title. Under each flap, write an example.
Step 3: Fill in the *Steps to Estimating Square Roots* piece. In each box, complete the step for estimating the $\sqrt{30}$. Cut out the piece. Apply glue to the back and attach it below the title.

Estimating Square Roots

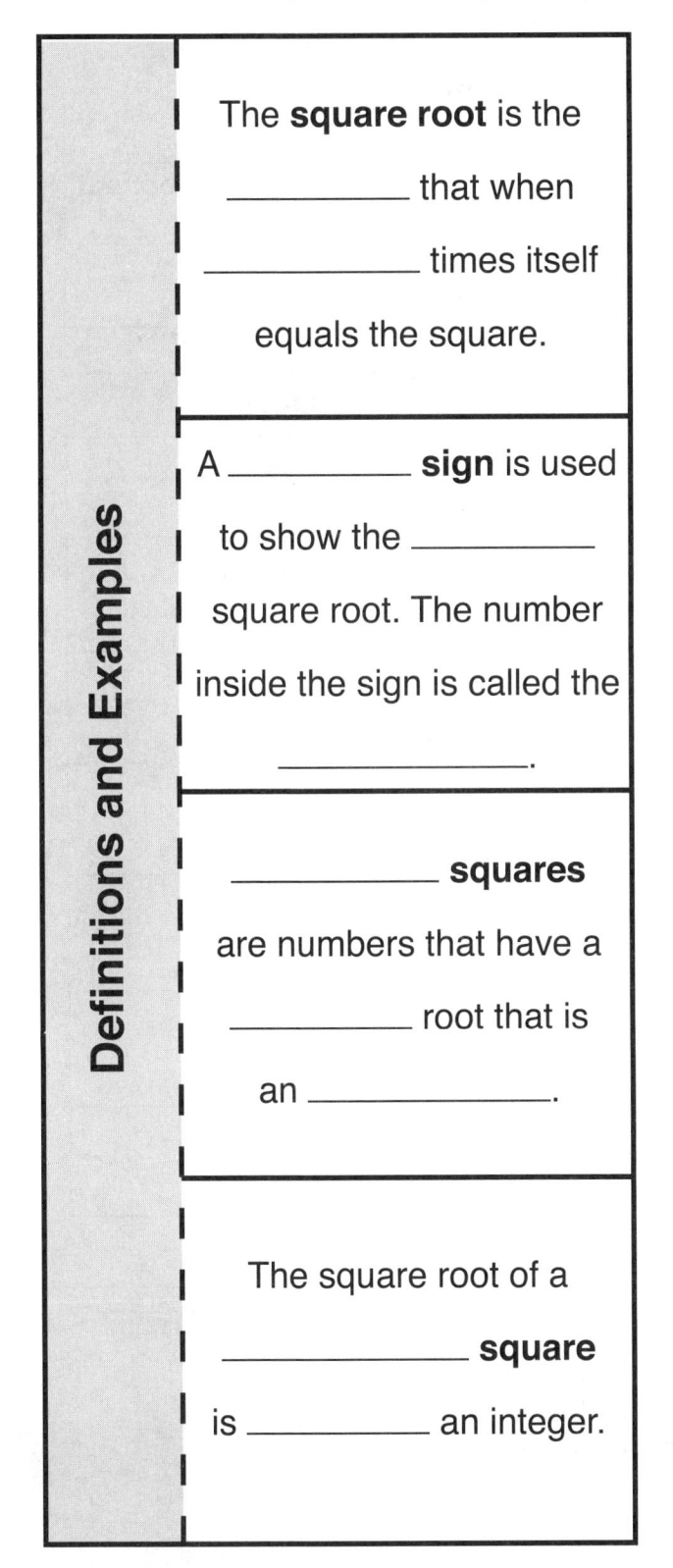

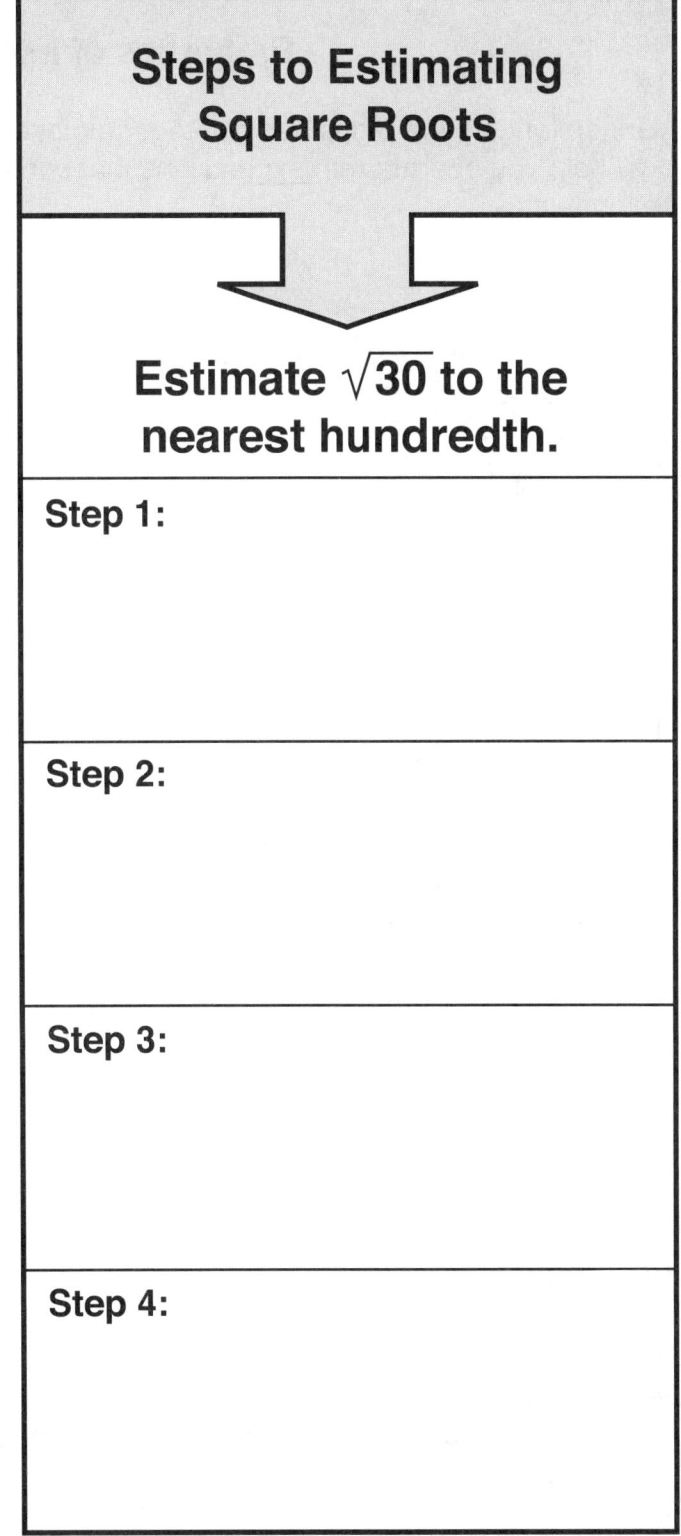

Definitions and Examples

The **square root** is the _____ that when _____ times itself equals the square.

A _____ **sign** is used to show the _____ square root. The number inside the sign is called the _____.

_____ **squares** are numbers that have a _____ root that is an _____.

The square root of a _____ **square** is _____ an integer.

Steps to Estimating Square Roots

Estimate $\sqrt{30}$ to the nearest hundredth.

Step 1:

Step 2:

Step 3:

Step 4:

Interactive Math Notebook: Grade 8   Student Instructions: Properties of Integer Exponents

Student Instructions: Properties of Integer Exponents

Read the following information. Cut out the mini-lesson and attach it to the right-hand page of your interactive notebook. Use what you have learned to create the left-hand page.

Mini-Lesson

Properties of Integer Exponents

Understanding the properties of integer exponents will help you operate with expressions that contain exponents.

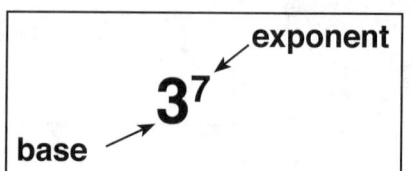

Property	Definition	Example
Product of a Power	Multiply base, add the exponents.	$x^2 \cdot x^3 = x^{2+3} = x^5$
Power of a Product	Apply the exponents to each factor and simplify.	$(4xy)^2 = 4^2 x^2 y^2$ $16x^2y^2$ Simplified
Power of a Power	Keep the base and multiply the exponents.	$(x^2)^3 = x^{2 \cdot 3} = x^6$
Quotient of Powers	Keep the base and subtract the exponents.	$\dfrac{x^3}{x^2} = x^{3-2} = x^1$ or x
Power of a Quotient	Apply the exponent to the numerator and denominator and simplify.	$\left(\dfrac{2m}{n}\right)^3 = \dfrac{2^3 \cdot m^3}{n^3} = \dfrac{8m^3}{n^3}$
Zero Power	Any nonzero quantity raised to a 0 exponent always equals 1.	$x^0 = 1$
Negative Power	Negative exponents produce positive fractions.	$x^{-2} = \dfrac{1}{x^2}$

Create Your Left-hand Notebook Page

Step 1: Cut out the title and glue it to the top of the notebook page.
Step 2: Cut out the *Properties of Integer Exponents* flap book. Apply glue to the back of the gray center section and attach it below the title.
Step 3: Under each flap, write the name of the property given.

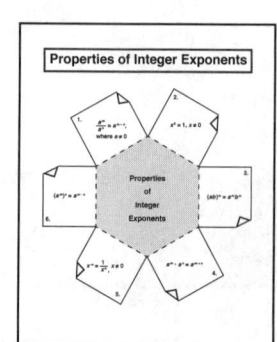

CD-405047 © Mark Twain Media, Inc., Publishers   10

Interactive Math Notebook: Grade 8 — Left-hand Page: Properties of Integer Exponents

Properties of Integer Exponents

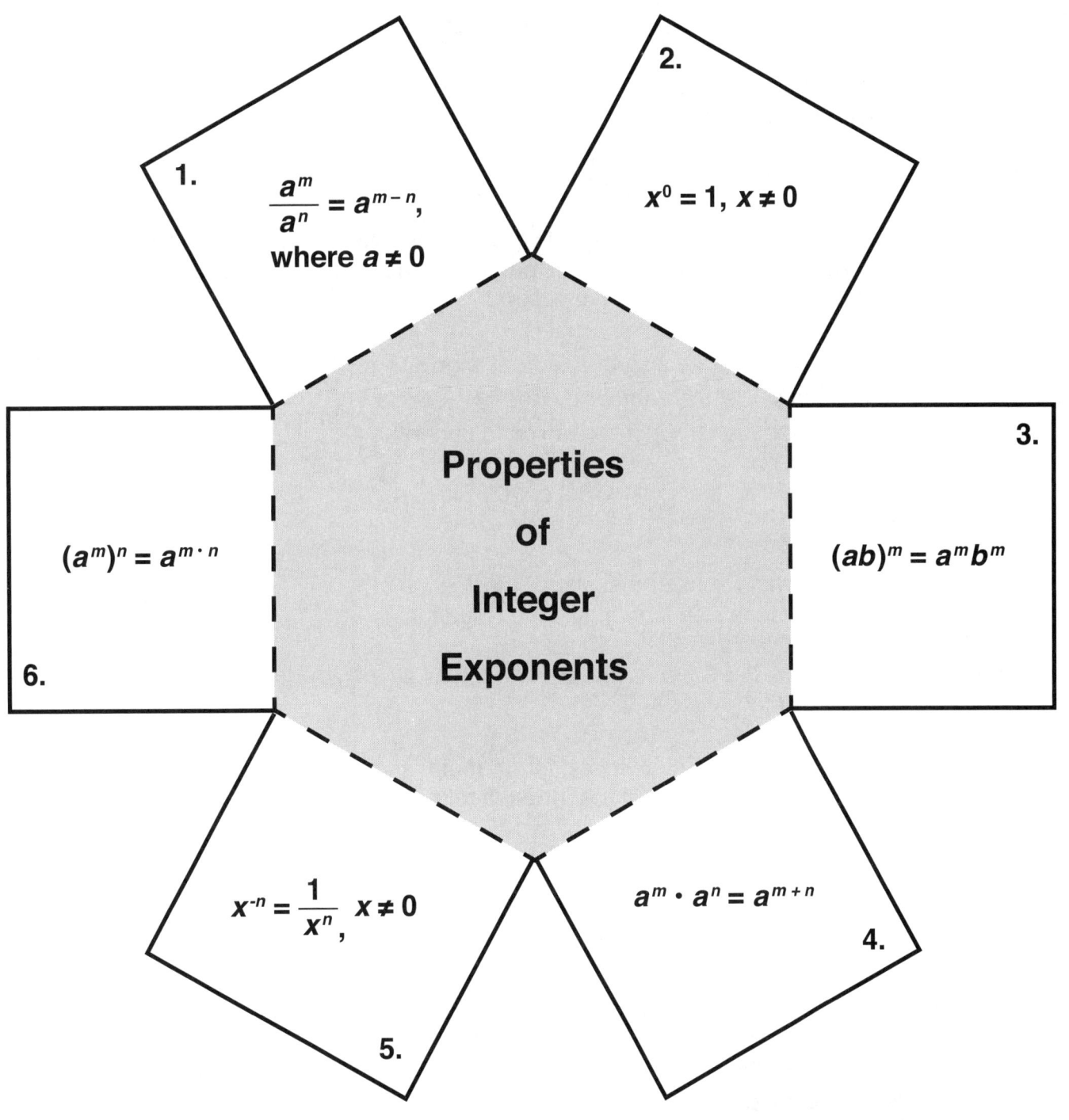

1. $\dfrac{a^m}{a^n} = a^{m-n}$, where $a \neq 0$

2. $x^0 = 1, x \neq 0$

3. $(ab)^m = a^m b^m$

4. $a^m \cdot a^n = a^{m+n}$

5. $x^{-n} = \dfrac{1}{x^n}, x \neq 0$

6. $(a^m)^n = a^{m \cdot n}$

Properties of Integer Exponents

Interactive Math Notebook: Grade 8   Student Instructions: Square Roots & Cube Roots

Student Instructions: Square Roots & Cube Roots

Read the following information. Cut out the mini-lesson and attach it to the right-hand page of your interactive notebook. Use what you have learned to create the left-hand page.

Mini-Lesson

Square Roots & Cube Roots

A **perfect square** is any whole number that shows the area of a square. The **square root** is the side length of the square. It is the value that is multiplied by itself.

$4^2 = 16$ $\sqrt{16} = 4$

Example: 4^2 and $4 \cdot 4 = 16$, so 4 (the side length) is the square root of 16.

Every number has two square roots: a positive and a negative. This is because when two negative numbers are multiplied together, their product is positive. In real-world situations, only the positive or **principal square root** is considered.

When you see the symbol $\sqrt{}$, it is the **radical sign**. The number under the radical is the **radicand**. The $\sqrt{}$ radical sign tells you to find the square root of the radicand under the radical sign.

radical → $\sqrt{36}$ ← radicand sign

Example: $\sqrt{16}$ means "find the square root of 16." Since 4^2, or $4 \cdot 4$, = 16, 4 is the square root of 16.

A **perfect cube** is any whole number that shows the volume of a cube. The **cube root** is the side length. It is the value that is multiplied by itself three times.

Example: 3^3 and $3 \cdot 3 \cdot 3 = 27$, so 3 (the side length) is a cube root of 27.

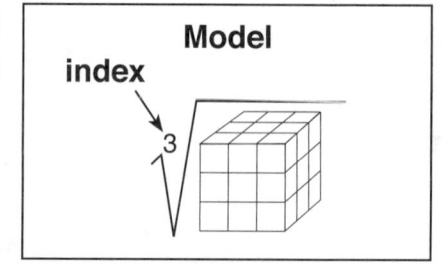

Many times you will need to find cube roots, fourth roots, and so on. The number above the radical is the **index**. It tells you the root to find.

Example: $\sqrt[3]{125}$ means "find the cube root of 125." Since 5^3, or $5 \cdot 5 \cdot 5 = 125$, 5 is the cube root of 125.

Create Your Left-hand Notebook Page

Step 1: Cut out the title and glue it to the top of the notebook page.
Step 2: Cut out the *What's the difference?* flap book. Apply glue to the gray center section and attach it below the title. Under each flap, write the definition.
Step 3: Complete the *Square Root Table* and *Cube Root Table* pieces. Find the perfect squares and cubes, and then find the square and cube roots. Cut out the pieces. Apply glue to the back of each and attach them below the title.

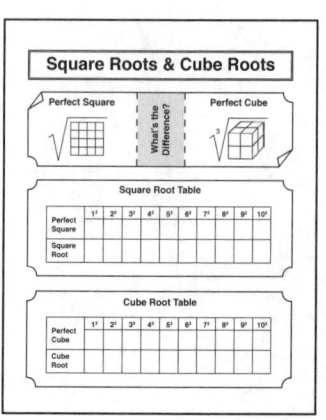

CD-405047 © Mark Twain Media, Inc., Publishers

Square Roots & Cube Roots

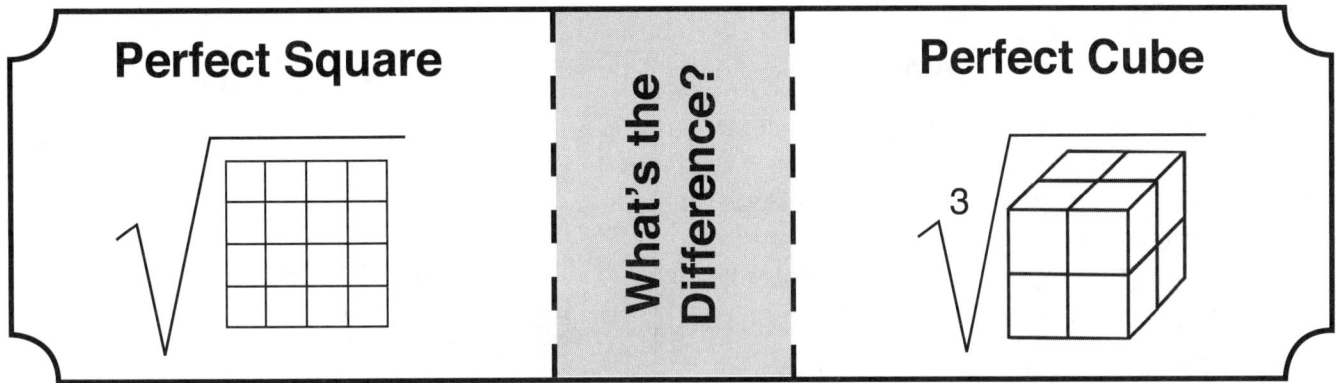

Square Root Table

Perfect Square	1^2	2^2	3^2	4^2	5^2	6^2	7^2	8^2	9^2	10^2
Square Root										

Cube Root Table

Perfect Cube	1^3	2^3	3^3	4^3	5^3	6^3	7^3	8^3	9^3	10^3
Cube Root										

Interactive Math Notebook: Grade 8   Student Instructions: Scientific Notation

Student Instructions: Scientific Notation

Read the following information. Cut out the mini-lesson and attach it to the right-hand page of your interactive notebook. Use what you have learned to create the left-hand page.

Mini-Lesson

Scientific Notation

Scientific notation is an expression used to represent a decimal number between 1 and 10 multiplied by a power of 10. Very large or small numbers can be written with fewer digits. Written $b \cdot 10^m$, *b* must **always** be greater than 1 and less than 10, and *m* is an integer.

Scientific Notation Rules
1. If a number is greater than or equal to 1, the exponent is positive.
   Example: $678{,}000{,}000 = 6.78 \times 10^7$
2. If the number is between 0 and 1, the exponent is negative.
   Example: $0.000000678 = 6.78 \times 10^{-7}$

Scientific Notation to Standard Form Notation
   Step 1: Move the decimal point to the left if the exponent of ten is a negative number.
   Step 2: Move the decimal point to the right if the exponent is positive.
   Step 3: Move the decimal point as many times as the exponent shows.

   Example: $2.7 \cdot 10^3 = 2{,}700$
   Positive exponent: move three places to the right. Add zeros for the extra place values. A decimal after a whole number is the same as a number without a decimal.

   Example: $3.25 \cdot 10^{-4} = 0.000325$
   Negative exponent: move four places to the left. Add zeros for the extra place values. A zero is placed before the decimal to show nothing in the one's place.

Standard Form Notation to Scientific Notation
   Step 1: Move the decimal point so that you have a number that is between 1 and 10. In a whole number, the decimal is at the end of the number.
   Step 2: Count the number of decimal places moved in step 1.
   Step 3: Write as a product of the number (found in step 1) and 10 raised to the power of the count.

   Example: Convert 4,645,000
   $\longrightarrow$ 4.645,000,
   $\longrightarrow$ $4.645 \cdot 10^6$

Create Your Left-hand Notebook Page
Step 1: Cut out the title and glue it to the top of the notebook page.
Step 2: Cut out the *Definition* and *Rules* flap books. Apply glue to the back of each gray tab and attach them below the title. Under the flaps, write the definition and the rules.
Step 3: Cut out the *Scientific Notation to Standard Form* and *Standard Form to Scientific Notation* flap books. Cut on the solid lines to create three flaps for each book. Apply glue to the back of each gray tab and attach them at the bottom of the page. Under each flap, write the answer.

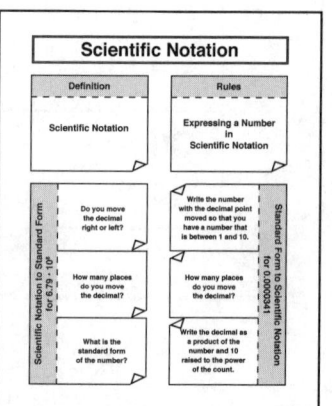

CD-405047 © Mark Twain Media, Inc., Publishers   14

Interactive Math Notebook: Grade 8 — Left-hand Page: Scientific Notation

Scientific Notation

Definition

Scientific Notation

Rules

Expressing a Number in Scientific Notation

Scientific Notation to Standard Form for $6.79 \cdot 10^8$

Do you move the decimal right or left?

How many places do you move the decimal?

What is the standard form of the number?

Standard Form to Scientific Notation for 0.0000341

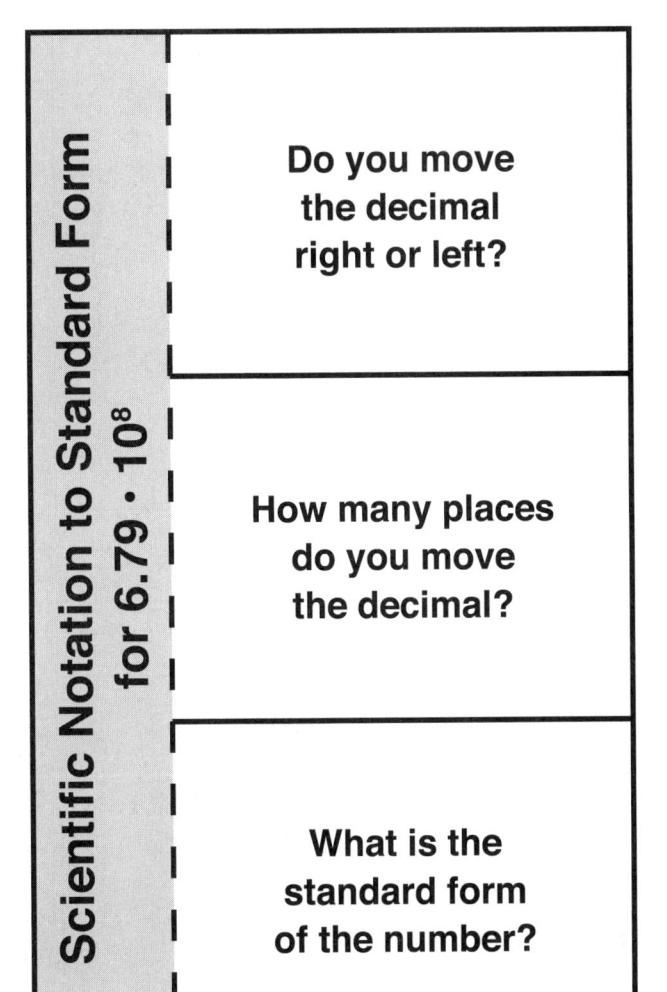

Write the number with the decimal point moved so that you have a number that is between 1 and 10.

How many places do you move the decimal?

Write the decimal as a product of the number and 10 raised to the power of the count.

CD-405047 © Mark Twain Media, Inc., Publishers

Interactive Math Notebook: Grade 8 — Student Instructions: Adding & Subtracting With Scientific Notation

Student Instructions: Adding & Subtracting With Scientific Notation

Read the following information. Cut out the mini-lesson and attach it to the right-hand page of your interactive notebook. Use what you have learned to create the left-hand page.

Mini-Lesson

Adding & Subtracting With Scientific Notation

You can add and subtract very large and small numbers that are written in scientific notation.

Adding and Subtracting in Scientific Notation
Examples: Exponents are the same
  Step 1: Add or subtract the coefficients (decimals) and keep the power of 10.
  Step 2: If needed, adjust the decimal and exponent so the answer is in scientific notation.

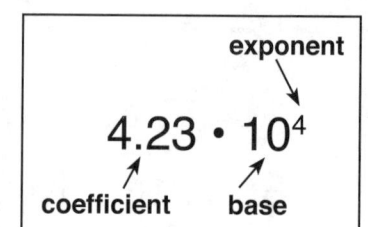

$$4.23 \cdot 10^4$$
coefficient — base — exponent

Addition	Subtraction
$(3.5 \cdot 10^4)$	$(8.9 \cdot 10^{-2})$
$+ (2.3 \cdot 10^4)$	$- (6.3 \cdot 10^{-2})$
$5.8 \cdot 10^4$	$2.6 \cdot 10^{-2}$

Examples: Exponents are different
  Step 1: Rewrite the decimal with the smaller exponent so that it has the same exponent as the decimal with the larger exponent by moving the decimal point.
  Step 2: Add/subtract the decimal numbers. The power of 10 will not change.
  Step 3: Give the answer in scientific notation. In the final answer, the coefficient must be between 1 and 10. Convert your result to scientific notation if necessary.

Add: $(5.02 \cdot 10^4) + (9.15 \cdot 10^5)$
  Step 1: $(.5.02 \cdot 10^5) + (9.15 \cdot 10^5)$
  Step 2: $(0.502 + 9.15) \cdot 10^5$
  Step 3: $9.652 \cdot 10^5$

Subtract: $(7.42 \cdot 10^8) - (1.253 \cdot 10^7)$
  Step 1: $(7.42 \cdot 10^8) - (.1.253 \cdot 10^8)$
  Step 2: $(7.42 - 0.1253) \cdot 10^8$
  Step 3: $7.2947 \cdot 10^8$

Create Your Left-hand Notebook Page

Step 1: Cut out the title and glue it to the top of the notebook page.
Step 2: Cut out the *Add and Subtract With Scientific Notation* flap book. Cut on the solid lines to create four flaps. Apply glue to the back of the gray center section and attach it below the title.
Step 3: Under each flap, add or subtract to give your answer in scientific notation.

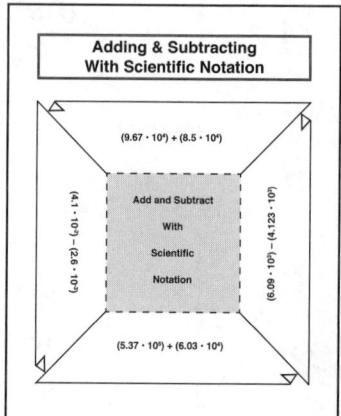

CD-405047 © Mark Twain Media, Inc., Publishers

Adding & Subtracting With Scientific Notation

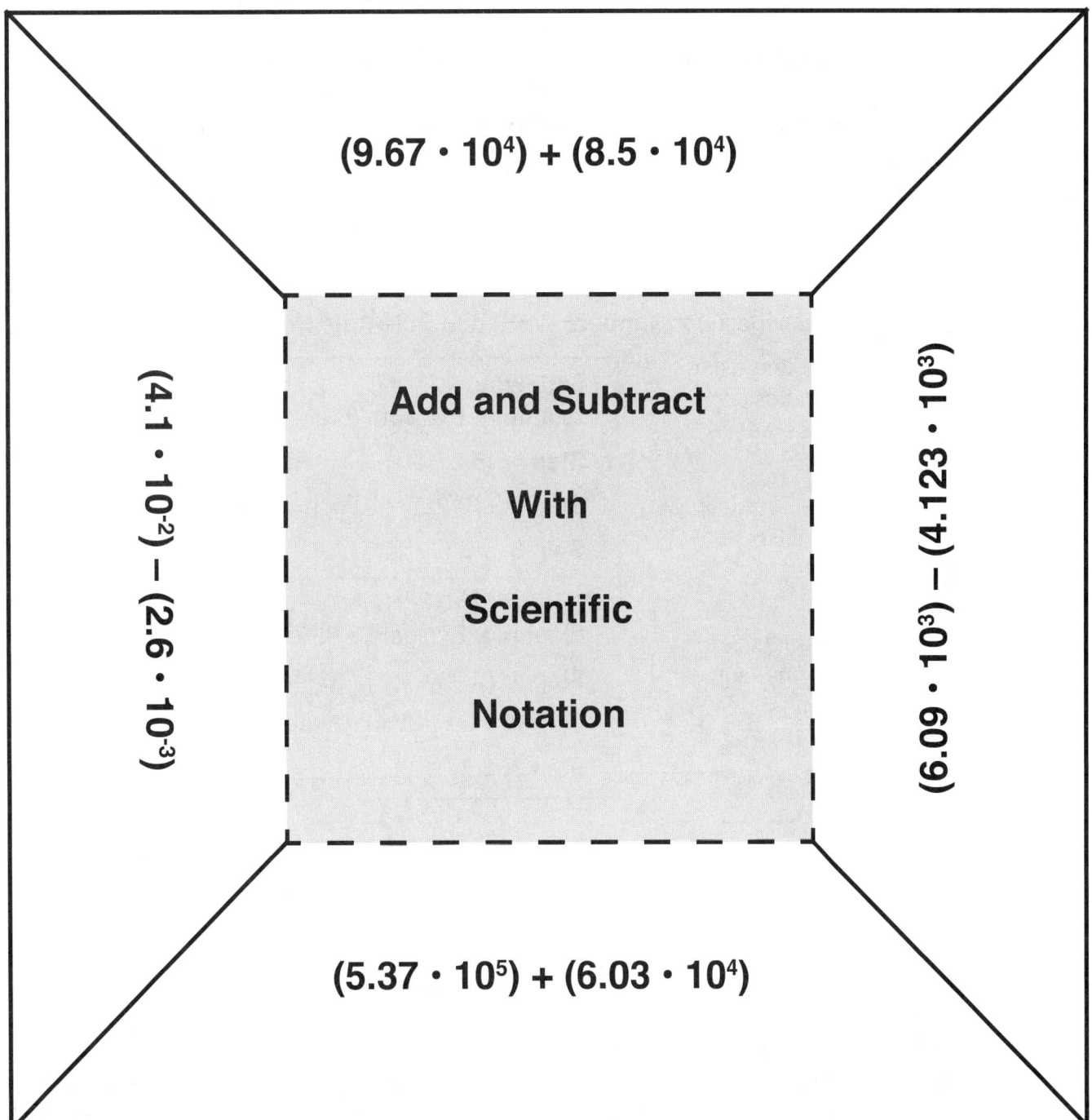

$(9.67 \cdot 10^4) + (8.5 \cdot 10^4)$

$(4.1 \cdot 10^{-2}) - (2.6 \cdot 10^{-3})$

Add and Subtract With Scientific Notation

$(6.09 \cdot 10^3) - (4.123 \cdot 10^3)$

$(5.37 \cdot 10^5) + (6.03 \cdot 10^4)$

Interactive Math Notebook: Grade 8   Student Instructions: Multiplying & Dividing With Scientific Notation

Student Instructions: Multiplying & Dividing With Scientific Notation

Read the following information. Cut out the mini-lesson and attach it to the right-hand page of your interactive notebook. Use what you have learned to create the left-hand page.

Mini-Lesson

Multiplying & Dividing With Scientific Notation

You can multiply and divide very large and small numbers that are written in scientific notation.

> **Rules for Multiplying and Dividing With Scientific Notation**
>
> **Rule 1:** When multiplying, multiply the coefficients (decimal numbers) and add the exponents.
>
> **Rule 2:** When dividing, divide the coefficients (decimal numbers) and subtract the exponents.

Steps to Multiply and Divide Two Numbers Written in Scientific Notation

Step 1: Rewrite the problem using commutative and/or associative properties.

Step 2: Follow the rules for multiplying or dividing scientific notation.

Step 3: Give the answer in scientific notation. In the final answer, the coefficient must be between 1 and 10.

> **Multiplying**
> **Example:** Evaluate $(6.2 \cdot 10^3)(3.1 \cdot 10^4)$.
> **Step 1:** $(6.2 \cdot 3.1) \cdot (10^3 \cdot 10^4) =$
> **Step 2:** $(19.22) \cdot (10^{3+4}) = 19.22 \cdot 10^7$
> **Step 3:** $1.922 \cdot 10^8$
>
> **Dividing**
> **Example:** Evaluate $7.98 \cdot 10^4 \div 2.1 \cdot 10^2$.
> **Step 1:** $(7.98 \div 2.1)(10^4 \div 10^2) =$
> **Step 2:** $3.8 \cdot (10^4 \div 10^2) = 3.8 \cdot 10^{4-2}$
> **Step 3:** $3.8 \cdot 10^2$

Create Your Left-hand Notebook Page

Step 1: Cut out the title and glue it to the top of the notebook page.

Step 2: Cut out the *Rules* flap book. Apply glue to the back of the gray center section and attach it below the title. Under each flap, write the rule.

Step 3: Cut out the *Multiply* and *Divide* flap books. Apply glue to the back of each gray center section and attach them at the bottom of the page. Under each *Step* flap, write the rule. Under each *Equation* flap, solve the problem.

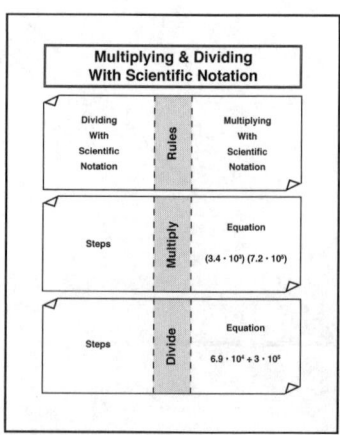

CD-405047 © Mark Twain Media, Inc., Publishers   18

Multiplying & Dividing With Scientific Notation

| Dividing With Scientific Notation | **Rules** | Multiplying With Scientific Notation |

| Steps | **Multiply** | Equation

$(3.4 \cdot 10^3)(7.2 \cdot 10^5)$ |

| Steps | **Divide** | Equation

$6.9 \cdot 10^4 \div 3 \cdot 10^5$ |

Interactive Math Notebook: Grade 8 Student Instructions: Solving Multi-Step Equations

Student Instructions: Solving Multi-Step Equations

Read the following information. Cut out the mini-lesson and attach it to the right-hand page of your interactive notebook. Use what you have learned to create the left-hand page.

Mini-Lesson

Solving Multi-Step Equations

An **equation** is a mathematical sentence showing two expressions are equal. Equations can be solved.

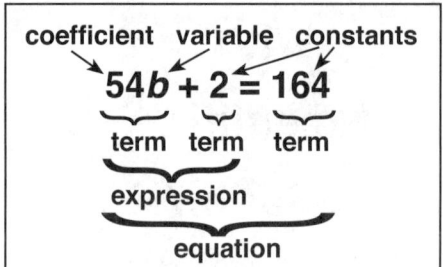

Parts of an Equation
- **Coefficient:** a number used to multiply a variable
- **Variable:** a symbol (letter of the alphabet) for a number we don't know
- **Constant:** a number on its own
- **Term:** either a single number or a variable, or numbers and variables multiplied together
- **Expression:** a sentence with a minimum of two numbers and at least one math operation

Multi-step equations take several steps to solve.

Tips
- Isolate the unknown variable on one side of the equation while keeping the constant on the opposite side.
- Keep the equation balanced. Whatever operation you perform on one side must also be applied on the other side.

Example: Solve $4(x + 2) - 10 = 2(x + 4)$.
- **Step 1:** Write the equation. ⟶ $4(x + 2) - 10 = 2(x + 4)$
- **Step 2:** Expand the expression using the Distributive Property. ⟶ $4x + 8 - 10 = 2x + 8$
- **Step 3:** Combine any like terms that are on the same side of the equation. ⟶ $4x - 2 = 2x + 8$
- **Step 4:** Collect all variables on one side of the equation. ⟶ $2x - 2 = 8$
- **Step 5:** Collect all constants on the opposite side of the variable. ⟶ $2x = 10$
- **Step 6:** Divide each side by the coefficient and simplify. ⟶ $x = 5$

Create Your Left-hand Notebook Page
- **Step 1:** Cut out the title and glue it to the top of the notebook page.
- **Step 2:** Label the *Parts of an Equation* piece, and list all the terms. Cut out the piece. Apply glue to the back and attach it below the title.
- **Step 3:** Cut out the *Which Step?* flap book. Apply glue to the back of the gray center section and attach it at the bottom of the page.
- **Step 4:** Under each flap, write the number of the step being described. Refer to the Student Instructions page if you need help.

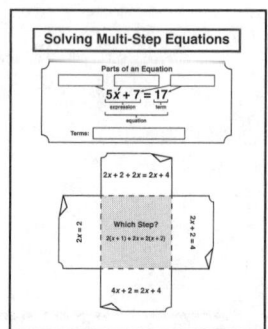

CD-405047 © Mark Twain Media, Inc., Publishers

Solving Multi-Step Equations

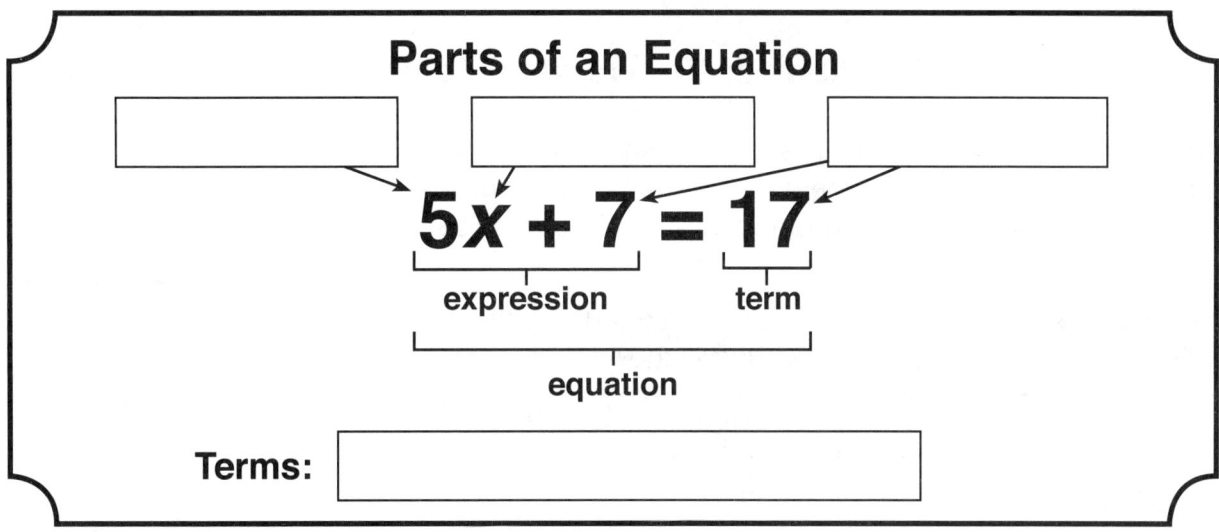

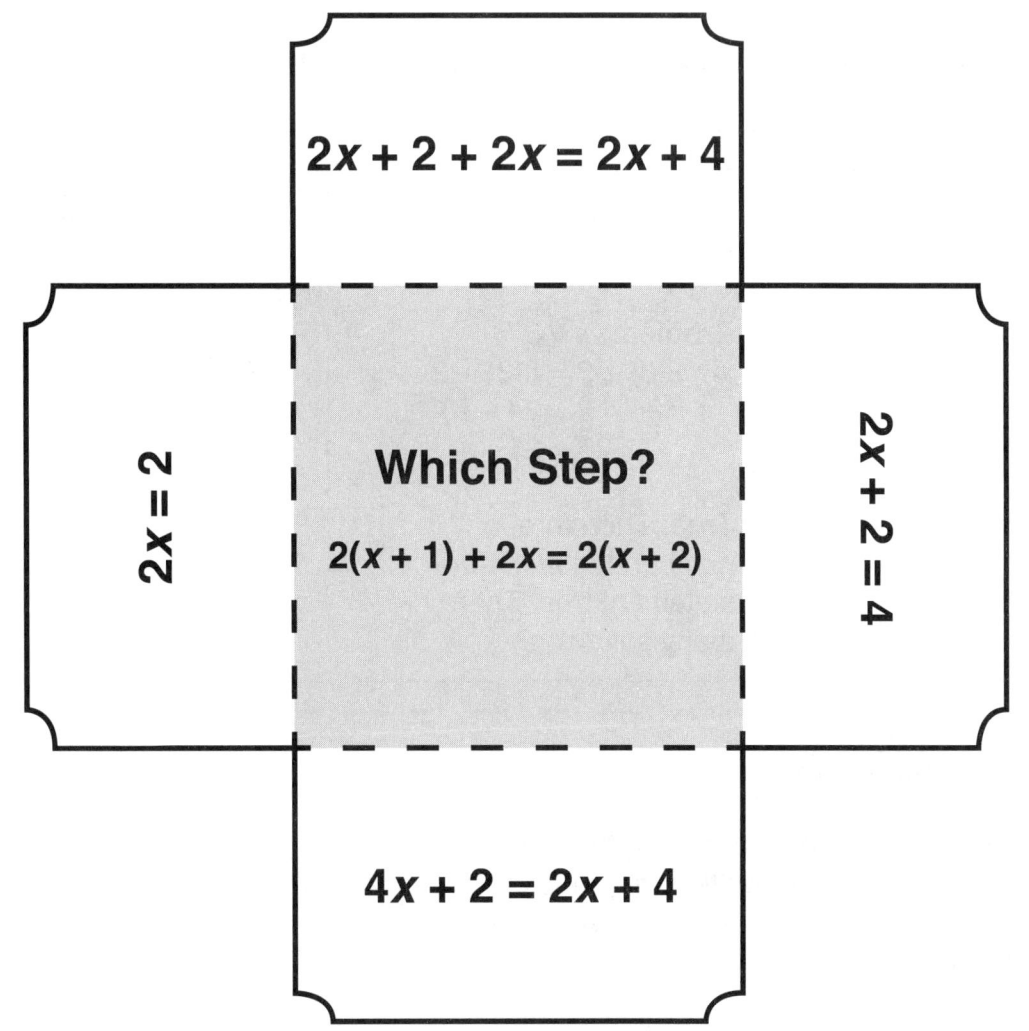

Interactive Math Notebook: Grade 8   Student Instructions: Solutions of One-Variable Equations

Student Instructions: Solutions of One-Variable Equations

Read the following information. Cut out the mini-lesson and attach it to the right-hand page of your interactive notebook. Use what you have learned to create the left-hand page.

Mini-Lesson

Solutions of One-Variable Equations

An **equation** is a mathematical sentence showing two expressions are equal. It consists of numbers and variables (letters like x or y) and operations ($+$, $-$, $\times$, $\div$). An equation contains an equal sign ($=$). Equations can be solved.

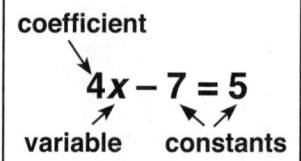
coefficient → $4x - 7 = 5$ ← variable, constants

Solving equations means to replace a variable with a value that results in a true statement. The **solution** is the value that replaced the variable in the equation.

Types of Solutions		
One Solution $x = a$ variable = constant	**Infinitely Many Solutions** $a = a$ constant = constant	**No Solutions** $a = b$ where $a \neq b$ constant = different constant
Example: $3x = 21$ $x = 7$	**Example:** $8x + 2 = 8x + 2$ $2 = 2$	**Example:** $5x + 4 = 5x$ $4 = 0$
There is only one solution that makes the equation a true statement.	Since 2 (constant) = 2 (constant), the solution is all numbers.	Since 4 (constant) ≠ 0 (different constant), there is no solution.
Problem: $x = 7$ $3x = 21$ $3(7) = 21$ $21 = 21$	**Problem:** $x = 3$ $8(3) + 2 = 8(3) + 2$ $24 + 2 = 24 + 2$ $26 = 26$	**Problem:** $x = 2$ $5(2) + 4 = 5(2)$ $10 + 4 = 10$ $14 \neq 10$
True: 7 is the only solution.	**True:** Therefore, any number can make the statement true. There are many solutions.	**False:** $14 \neq 10$, therefore, there is no number that will make this statement true. There is no solution.

Your Left-hand Notebook Page

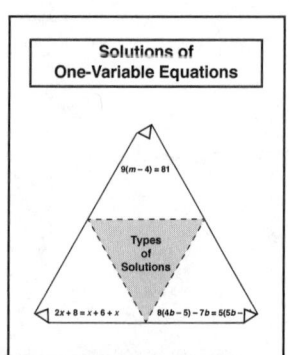

Step 1: Cut out the title and glue it to the top of the notebook page.
Step 2: Cut out the *Types of Solutions* flap book. Apply glue to the gray center section and attach it below the title.
Step 3: Under each flap, solve the equation and write the type of solution.

Interactive Math Notebook: Grade 8 — Left-hand Page: Solutions of One-Variable Equations

Solutions of One-Variable Equations

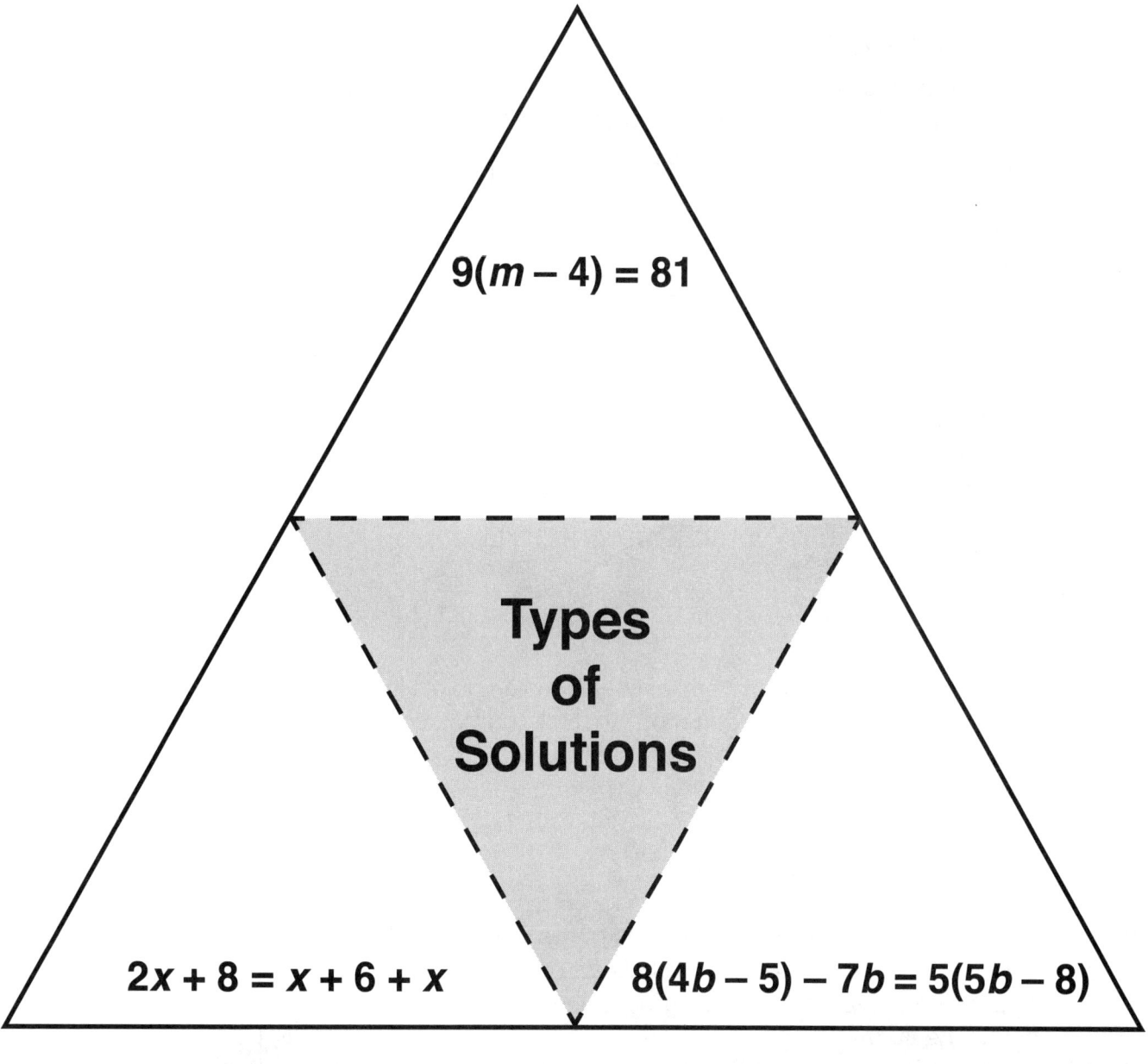

$9(m - 4) = 81$

Types of Solutions

$2x + 8 = x + 6 + x$ $8(4b - 5) - 7b = 5(5b - 8)$

Interactive Math Notebook: Grade 8   Student Instructions: Solving Systems of Equations Graphically

Student Instructions: Solving Systems of Equations Graphically

Read the following information. Cut out the mini-lesson and attach it to the right-hand page of your interactive notebook. Use what you have learned to create the left-hand page.

Mini-Lesson

Solving Systems of Equations Graphically

A set of two or more equations that contain two or more of the same variables is a **system of equations**. The solution of a system of equations is a set of ordered pairs (x, y) that make all of the equations in a system true.

To solve a system of linear equations graphically, we graph both equations in the same coordinate system. The graph of a system of equations shows the number of solutions.

Examples: Solve each system by graphing.

$y = 2x + 2$ $y = -\frac{1}{2}x + 4$ $2x - y = 4$
$y = x - 1$ $y = -\frac{1}{2}x - 6$ $6x - 3y = 12$

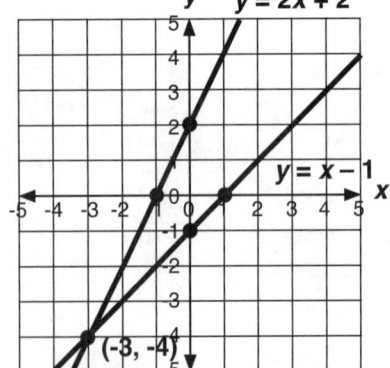 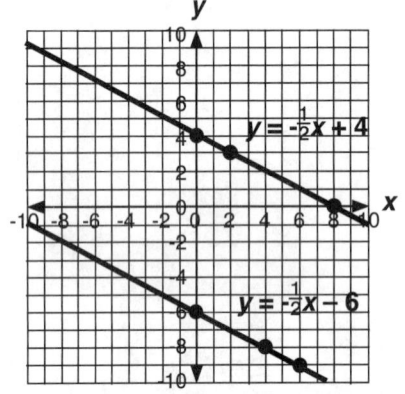 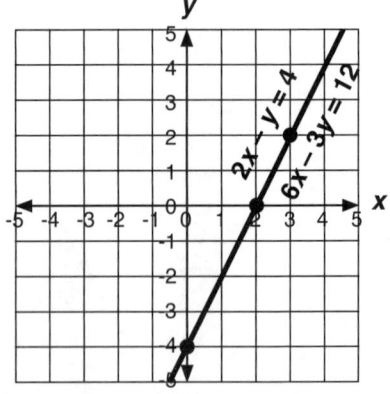

Intersecting lines have one point in common; there is one solution to this system. Solution is (-3, -4).

Parallel lines have no points in common; there is no solution to this system.

Both equations give the same line; there are infinitely many solutions.

Create Your Left-hand Notebook Page

Step 1: Cut out the title and glue it to the top of the notebook page.
Step 2: Cut out the 3 flap books: *Graph 1*, *Graph 2*, and *Graph 3*. Apply glue to the back of each gray tab and attach them below the title.
Step 3: Under each flap, explain how the system of equations supports the solution.

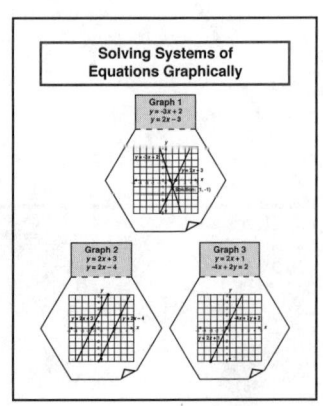

Interactive Math Notebook: Grade 8 — Left-hand Page: Solving Systems of Equations Graphically

Solving Systems of Equations Graphically

Graph 1
$y = -3x + 2$
$y = 2x - 3$

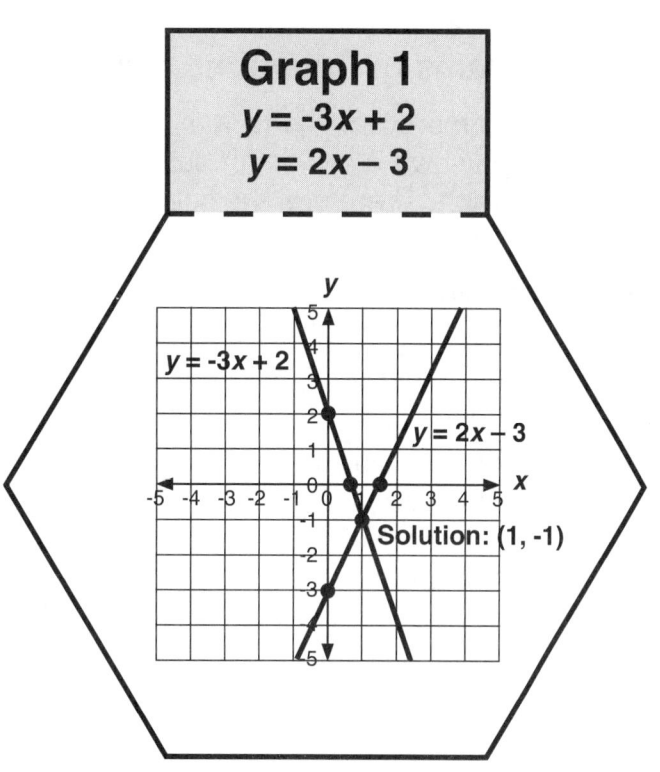

Graph 2
$y = 2x + 3$
$y = 2x - 4$

Graph 3
$y = 2x + 1$
$-4x + 2y = 2$

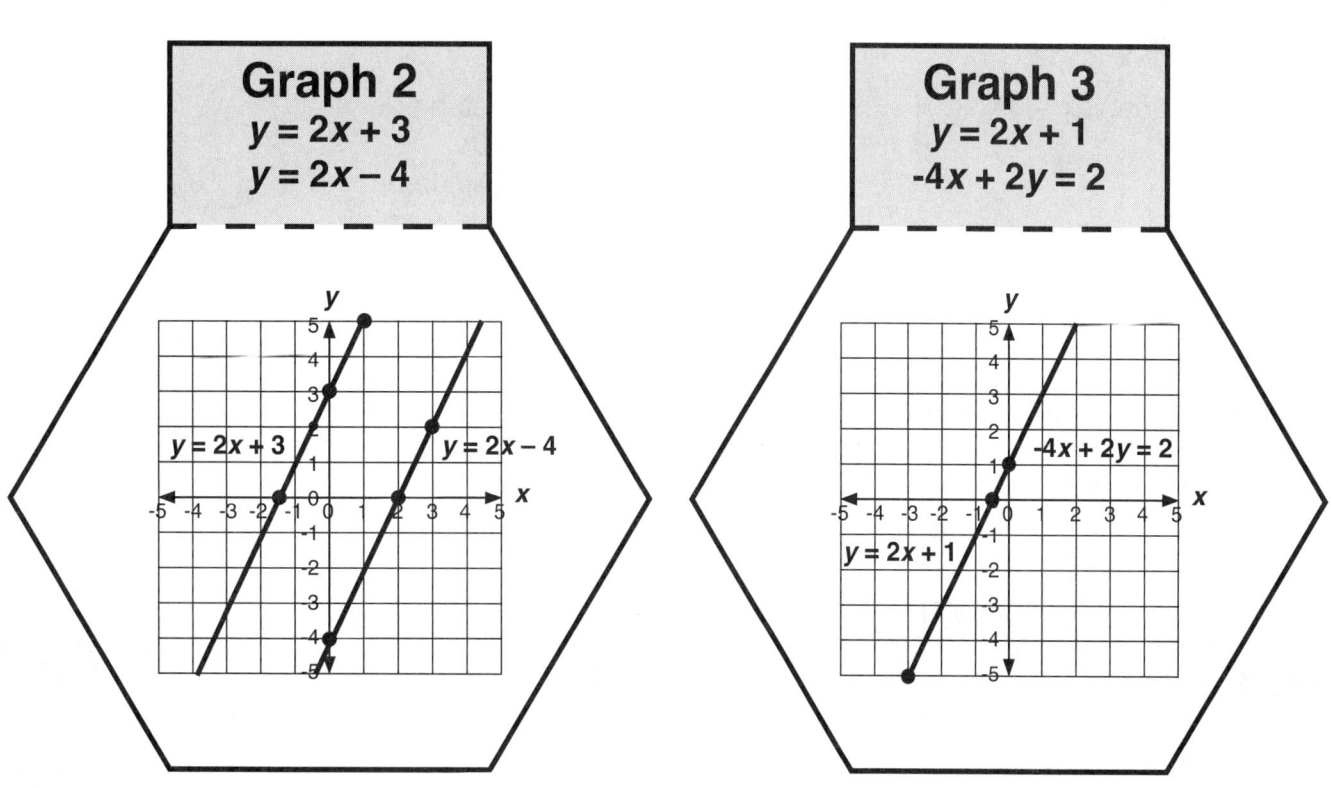

Interactive Math Notebook: Grade 8   Student Instructions: Solving Systems of Equations Algebraically

Student Instructions: Solving Systems of Equations Algebraically

Read the following information. Cut out the mini-lesson and attach it to the right-hand page of your interactive notebook. Use what you have learned to create the left-hand page.

Mini-Lesson

Solving Systems of Equations Algebraically

A **system of equations** is two or more equations with the same set of unknown values. **Substitution** is an algebraic way to solve a system of equations. What you are finding is the point where two lines cross on a graph. Therefore, the solution to the system of equations will be an ordered pair, (x, y).

Example: Solve the system of equations algebraically.
$y = 2x$ ← First equation y has the exact same value as $2x$, they just look different.
$y = x + 5$ ← Second equation   This means that you can replace y in the second equation with $2x$.

$2x = x + 5$ ← Now, you only have 1 variable and can actually solve.
$2x - x = x - x$ ← Subtract an x from each side.
$x = 5$ ← $x = 5$. So, you have found the x value.
$y = 2 \cdot 5$ or $y = 5 + 5$ ← Insert the x value (5) into either equation to find y.
$y = 10$ ← The value of y is 10.
So, the solution to this system (x, y) is $(5, 10)$.

Example: Solve the system of equations algebraically.
$x = 2y - 4$ ← First equation x has the same value as $2y - 4$, so take out x in the second
$x + 8y = 16$ ← Second equation   equation and replace it with $2y - 4$ and bring down the rest of the problem.

New equation: $2y - 4 + 8y = 16$ Now, solve the multi-step equation.
$10y - 4 = 16$ ← Combine $2y + 8y = 10y$.
$10y = 20$ ← Add 4 to each side. Divide each side by 10.
$y = 2$ ← So, you have found the y value.
$x = 2 \cdot 2 - 4$ ← Insert the y value into either equation to find x.
$x = 0$ So, the solution to this system (x, y) is $(0, 2)$.

Create Your Left-hand Notebook Page
Step 1: Cut out the title and glue it to the top of the notebook page.
Step 2: Fill in the blanks on the *System of Equations* piece. Cut out the piece. Apply glue to the back and attach it below the title.
Step 3: Fill in the blanks on the *Solving Systems of Equations* piece. Cut out the piece. Apply glue to the back and attach it below the *System of Equations* piece.
Step 4: Cut out the *Solve the System* flap book. Apply glue to the back of the gray center section and attach it at the bottom of the page. Under each flap, solve the system of equations.

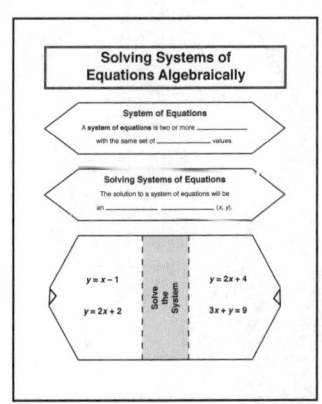

CD-405047 © Mark Twain Media, Inc., Publishers   26

Solving Systems of Equations Algebraically

System of Equations

A **system of equations** is two or more _____ with the same set of _____ values.

Solving Systems of Equations

The solution to a system of equations will be an _____ _____, (x, y).

$y = x - 1$

$y = 2x + 2$

Solve the System

$y = 2x + 4$

$3x + y = 9$

Interactive Math Notebook: Grade 8 — Student Instructions: Graphing Proportional Relationships

Student Instructions: Graphing Proportional Relationships

Read the following information. Cut out the mini-lesson and attach it to the right-hand page of your interactive notebook. Use what you have learned to create the left-hand page.

Mini-Lesson

Graphing Proportional Relationships

Ordered pairs are a pair of numbers (*x*, *y*) used to plot a point on a coordinate plane. Graphing ordered pairs is a way to visually represent the proportional relationship between the values of the *x*-variable and the *y*-variable. The values that you input (insert) for *x* will determine the output or amount of change in the values of *y*.

A **proportional relationship** has a constant ratio between the *x* and *y* variables called the **constant of proportionality**. This constant represents the rate of change, which is the ratio of the amount of change in the output to the amount of change in the input. The equation for a proportional relationship can be expressed in the form **y = kx**, where *k* is the constant of proportionality. Use tables and graphs to test for proportional relationships.

Tables and Graphs
  Example: A snail travels 5 inches every 1 hour.

Table

Hours Input x	Relationship y = 5x	Inches Output y
0	y = 5(0)	0
1	y = 5(1)	5
2	y = 5(2)	10
3	y = 5(3)	15
4	y = 5(4)	20

Graph

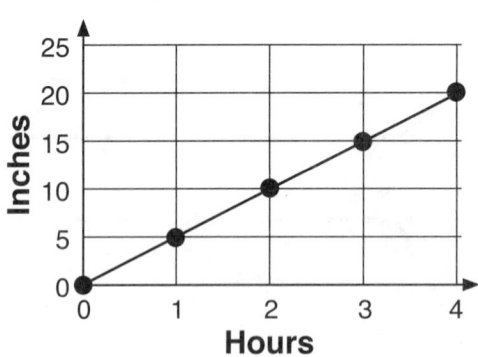

The constant rate of change is $\frac{5}{1}$ or 5, so the table represents a proportional relationship.

The points form a straight line. The line goes through the origin, so the graph represents a proportional relationship.

Create Your Left-hand Notebook Page
Step 1: Cut out the title and glue it to the top of the notebook page.
Step 2: Fill in the blanks on the *Proportional Relationships* piece. Cut out the piece. Apply glue to the back and attach it below the title.
Step 3: Use the table to graph the (*x*, *y*) pairs on the *Testing Proportional Relationships* flap book. Cut out the flap book. Apply glue to the back of the gray tab and attach it at the bottom of the page. Under the flap, tell if the relationship represents a proportional relationship. Explain your answer.

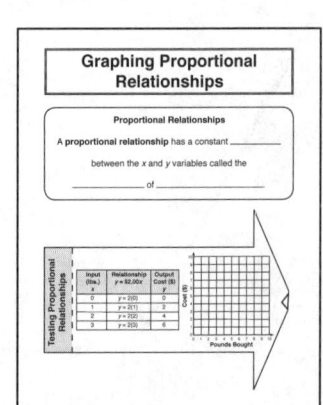

CD-405047 © Mark Twain Media, Inc., Publishers

Graphing Proportional Relationships

Proportional Relationships

A **proportional relationship** has a constant _____

between the *x* and *y* variables called the

_____ of _____.

Testing Proportional Relationships

Input (lbs.) *x*	Relationship *y* = $2.00*x*	Output Cost ($) *y*
0	*y* = 2(0)	0
1	*y* = 2(1)	2
2	*y* = 2(2)	4
3	*y* = 2(3)	6

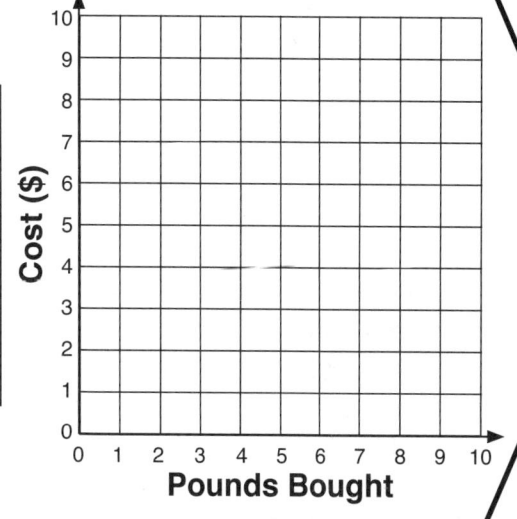

Interactive Math Notebook: Grade 8   Student Instructions: Slope of a Line

Student Instructions: Slope of a Line

Read the following information. Cut out the mini-lesson and attach it to the right-hand page of your interactive notebook. Use what you have learned to create the left-hand page.

Mini-Lesson

Slope of a Line

When you plot two points on a coordinate plane and connect them with a straight line, you will create a **linear graph**. The steepness of the line is called the **slope** (also referred to as rate of change). The type of slope can be identified as positive or negative.

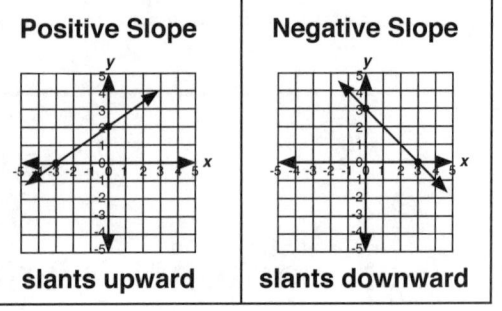

The slope of a line can be expressed as a ratio comparing the value of two points on a graph. The slope is simply the ratio of the rise to run. The **rise** is the "change in *y*" or how many units up or down the line travels on the graph between the points. The **run** is the "change in *x*" or the distance left or right the line travels.

Ratio

$$\text{slope} = \frac{\text{rise}}{\text{run}}$$

You can find the slope of a line by counting rise to run units from point to point on a graph.

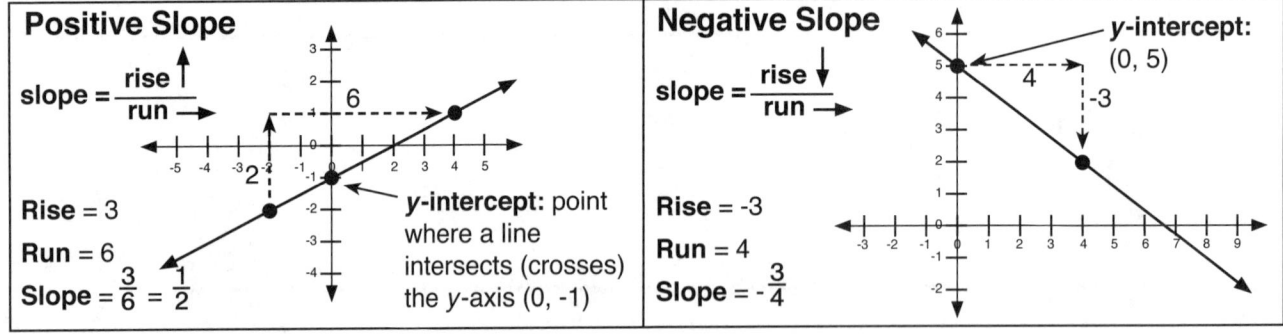

A **linear equation** is an equation between two variables that gives a straight line when plotted on a graph. Every straight line can be represented by the linear equation: $y = mx + b$.

$y = mx + b$ → • *y*-intercept

- dependent variable
- *y*-coordinate in ordered pair

- slope
- rate of change

- independent variable
- *x*-coordinate in ordered pair

Create Your Left-hand Notebook Page

Step 1: Cut out the title and glue it to the top of the notebook page.

Step 2: Cut out the *Linear Formula* flap book. Cut on the solid lines to create four flaps. Apply glue to the back of the gray center section and attach it below the title. Under each flap, write the part of the formula described.

Step 3: Cut out the *Linear Graph* flap book. Cut on the solid lines to create four flaps. Apply glue to the back of the gray center section and attach it at the bottom of the page. Determine the type of slope, slope ratio, *y*-intercept, and slope for the graph. Write your answer under the correct flap.

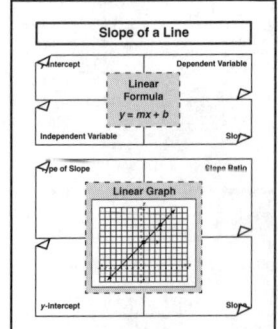

CD-405047 © Mark Twain Media, Inc., Publishers

Interactive Math Notebook: Grade 8 — Left-hand Page: Slope of a Line

Slope of a Line

y-intercept	Dependent Variable
Independent Variable	Slope

Linear Formula
$$y = mx + b$$

Type of Slope	Slope Ratio
y-intercept	Slope

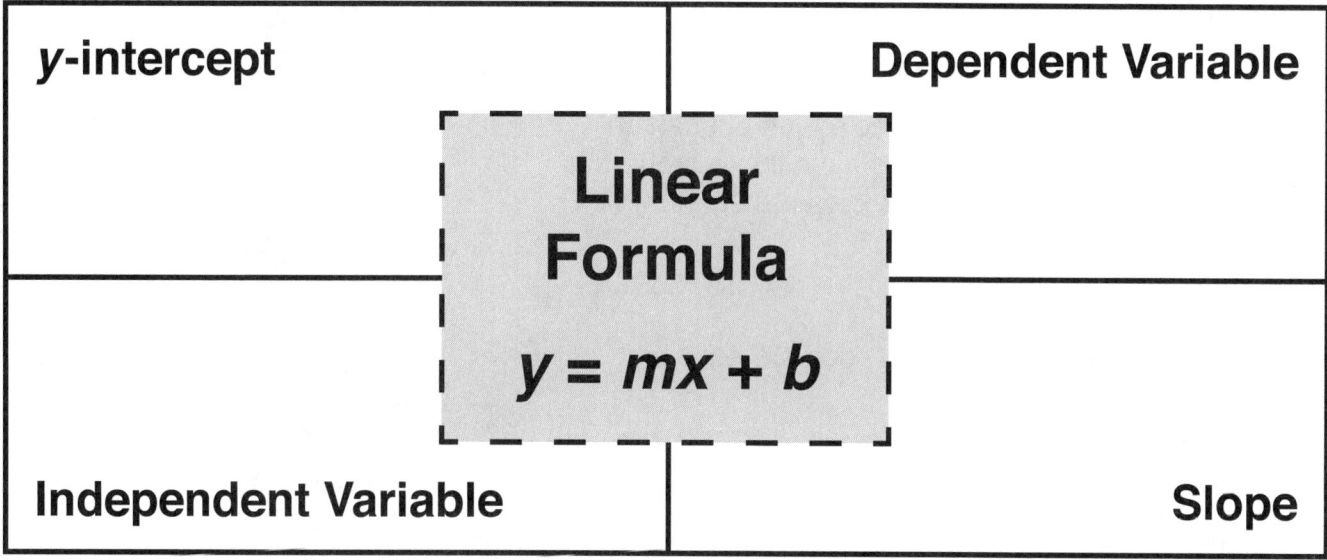

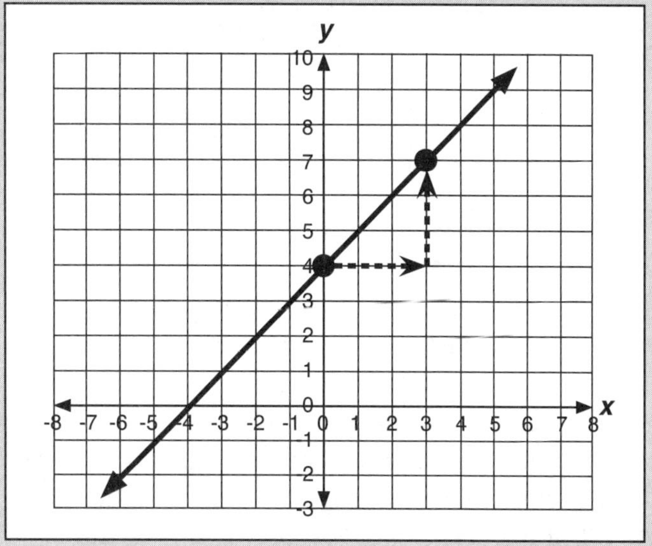

Linear Graph

CD-405047 © Mark Twain Media, Inc., Publishers

Interactive Math Notebook: Grade 8 — Student Instructions: Similar Triangles & Slope

Student Instructions: Similar Triangles & Slope

Read the following information. Cut out the mini-lesson and attach it to the right-hand page of your interactive notebook. Use what you have learned to create the left-hand page.

Mini-Lesson

Similar Triangles & Slope

Similar triangles have the same shape but can be different sizes. Similar triangles have these properties:
- Corresponding interior angles are equal:
  $\angle A = \angle D$
  $\angle B = \angle E$
  $\angle C = \angle F$
- Ratios of corresponding sides are equal:
  $\dfrac{AB}{DE} = \dfrac{BC}{EF} = \dfrac{CA}{FD}$

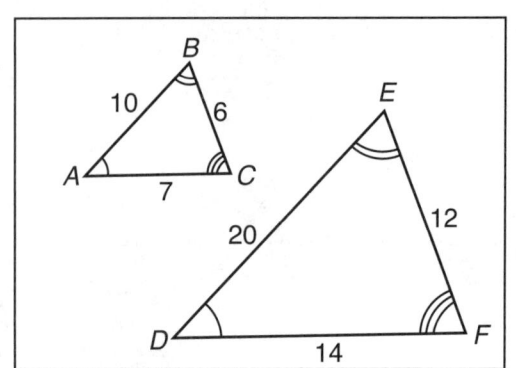

A line is graphed on a coordinate plane; the **slope** is a measure of its steepness. Similar right triangles can be used to illustrate slope. To find slope, use the formula: **slope** $= \dfrac{\text{change in } y}{\text{change in } x}$. So, divide the change in height (y) of the triangle by the change in horizontal distance (x).

Example 1:

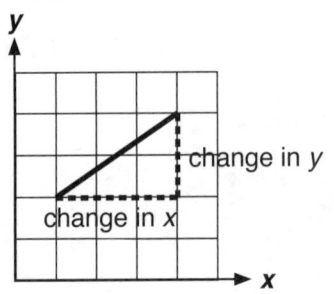

slope $= \dfrac{\text{change in } y}{\text{change in } x} = \dfrac{y_2 - y_1}{x_2 - x_1}$

Example 2:

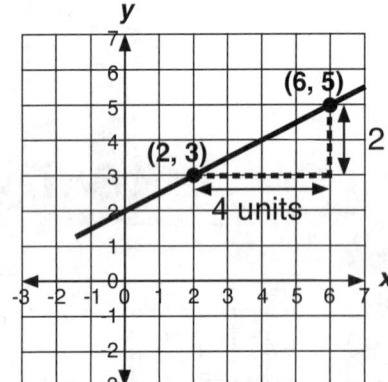

slope $= \dfrac{5-3}{6-2} = \dfrac{2}{4} = 0.5$

Create Your Left-hand Notebook Page

Step 1: Cut out the title and glue it to the top of the notebook page.

Step 2: Cut out the *Similar Triangles* flap book. Cut on the solid line to create two flaps. Apply glue to the back of the gray tab and attach it below the title. Under the flap, write the corresponding angles and the ratios of the corresponding sides.

Step 3: Cut out the *Slope* flap book. Apply glue to the back of the gray tab and attach it at the bottom of the page. Under the flap, find the slope. Show your work.

Step 4: Cut out the *Similar Triangle Properties* and *Slope* pieces. Apply glue to the back of each piece and attach them on the right side of the page.

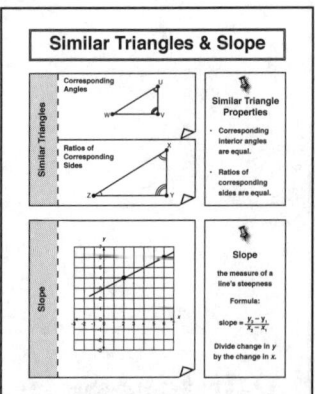

CD-405047 © Mark Twain Media, Inc., Publishers

Similar Triangles & Slope

Similar Triangles

Corresponding Angles

Ratios of Corresponding Sides

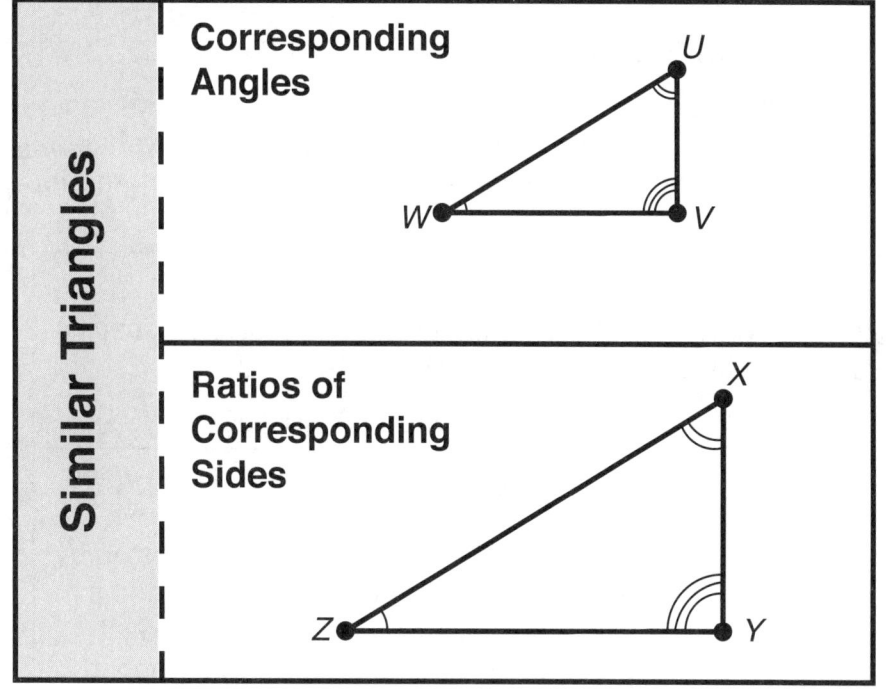

Similar Triangle Properties

- Corresponding interior angles are equal.

- Ratios of corresponding sides are equal.

Slope

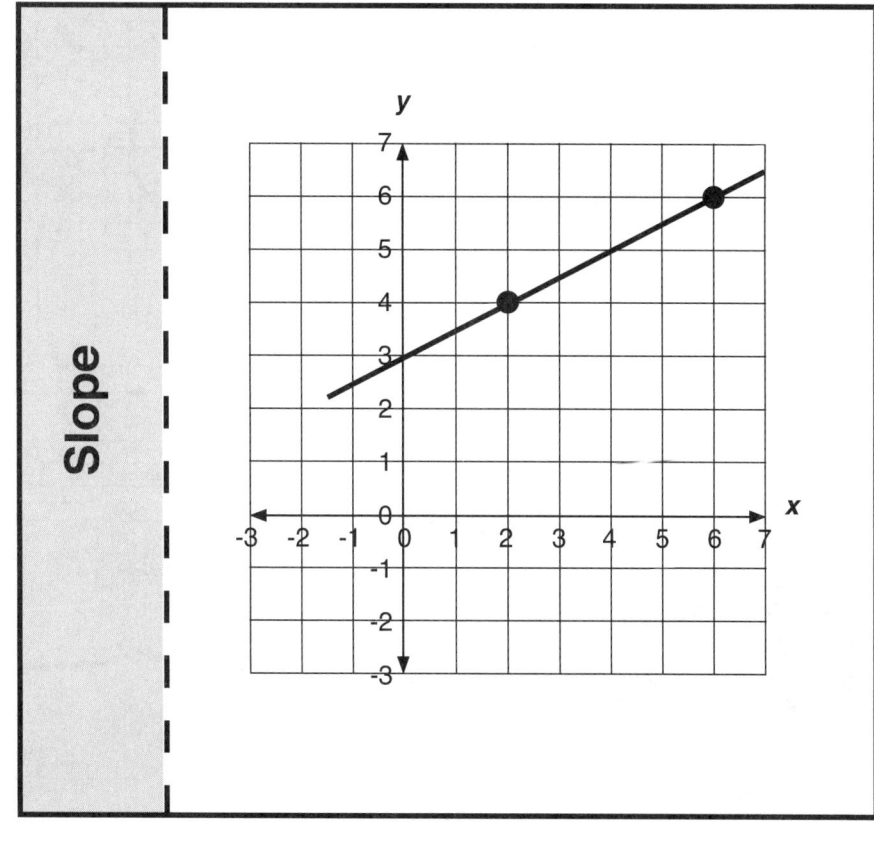

Slope

the measure of a line's steepness

Formula:

$$\text{slope} = \frac{y_2 - y_1}{x_2 - x_1}$$

Divide change in *y* by the change in *x*.

Interactive Math Notebook: Grade 8   Student Instructions: Functions

Student Instructions: Functions

Read the following information. Cut out the mini-lesson and attach it to the right-hand page of your interactive notebook. Use what you have learned to create the left-hand page.

Mini-Lesson

Functions

A **function** represents a special relationship between two ordered pairs (x, y). In a function, x represents the **input** (independent variable) and y represents the **output** (dependent variable). Every function has only one output for each input. Another word for input is **domain** and for output is **range**.

Equation: $y = f(x)$

A **function rule** is an equation that compares the input to the output. When given a specific value for x, the equation has only one answer for y.

Function: $y = 2x + 2$ or $y = x^2 - 1$ **Not a Function:** $y^2 = x + 5$

Function Table: A table represents a function when none of the independent values (x) are repeated. There is only one corresponding y value for each x value.

Pot Holders	
Input	Output
x	y
1	2
2	4
3	6
4	8

Function

Pot Holders	
Input	Output
x	y
3	1
5	2
3	3
3	5

Not a Function

Graph: A graph represents a function when there is only one y value for each corresponding x value. This can be tested by drawing a vertical line on the graph, and if it hits the graphed line in only one spot, it represents a function. If it hits the graph in more than one spot, then it is not a function.

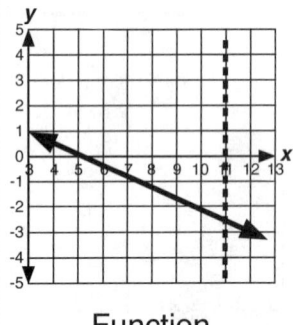
Function

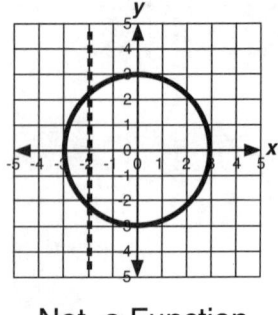
Not a Function

Create Your Left-hand Notebook Page

Step 1: Cut out the title and glue it to the top of the notebook page.
Step 2: Complete the *Does It Represent a Function?* chart. Determine if the equation, table, or graph represents a function and explain your answer.
Step 3: Cut out the chart. Apply glue to the back and attach it below the title.

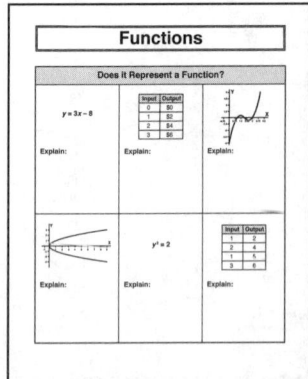

CD-405047 © Mark Twain Media, Inc., Publishers   34

Interactive Math Notebook: Grade 8 — Left-hand Page: Functions

Functions

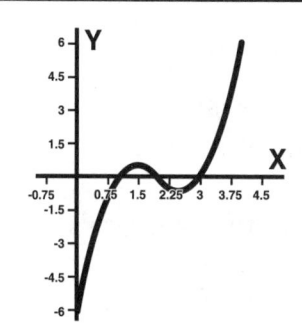

Does it Represent a Function?

$y = 3x - 8$ Explain:	Input / Output table: 0 → $0 1 → $2 2 → $4 3 → $6 Explain:	Graph (curve) Explain:
Graph (sideways parabola) Explain:	$y^2 = 2$ Explain:	Input / Output table: 1 → 2 2 → 4 1 → 5 3 → 6 Explain:

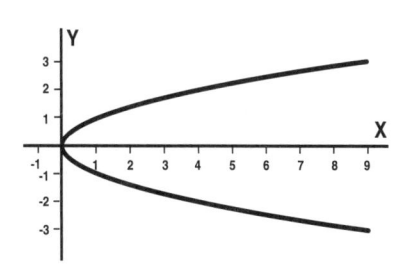

CD-405047 © Mark Twain Media, Inc., Publishers

Interactive Math Notebook: Grade 8

Student Instructions: Rate of Change

Read the following information. Cut out the mini-lesson and attach it to the right-hand page of your interactive notebook. Use what you have learned to create the left-hand page.

Mini-Lesson

Rate of Change

Rate of change is a function that describes how one quantity changes in relation to another quantity. Graphs and tables can be used to represent rate of change.

Graphically
Points on the coordinate plane can be used to find the rate of change.

Rate of Change Formula: $\dfrac{y_2 - y_1}{x_2 - x_1}$

A Snail's Pace

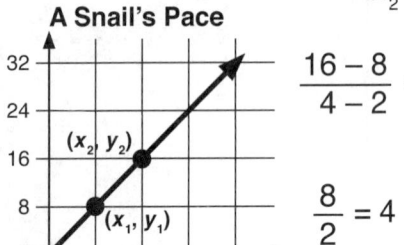

$\dfrac{16 - 8}{4 - 2} =$

Step 1: Choose any two points from the graph and plug the values in the formula. Let (2, 8) be (x_1, y_1) and (4, 16) be (x_2, y_2).

$\dfrac{8}{2} = 4$

Step 2: Simplify.

The rate of change is 4. This means a snail is traveling at a rate of 4 ft. per hour.

Table
A table gives us a list of input values and their corresponding output values, which can be used to find rate of change.

Rate of Change Formula: $\dfrac{y_2 - y_1}{x_2 - x_1}$

| Money Saved ||
Months Input x	Money Output y
3	10
4	30
5	50
6	70

$\dfrac{50 - 10}{5 - 3} =$

Step 1: Choose any two points from the table and plug the values in the formula. Let (3, 10) be (x_1, y_1) and (5, 50) be (x_2, y_2)

$\dfrac{40}{2} = 20$

Step 2: Simplify.

The rate of change is 20. This means the amount saved each month is $20.

Create Your Left-hand Notebook Page
Step 1: Cut out the title and glue it to the top of the notebook page.
Step 2: Fill in the blanks on the *Definition* piece. Cut out the piece. Apply glue to the back and attach it below the title.
Step 3: Write the rate of change formula on the *Formula* piece. Cut out the piece. Apply glue to the back and attach it below the title.
Step 4: Find the rate of change for the *Graph* and *Table* pieces. Cut out both pieces. Apply glue to the backs and attach them at the bottom of the page.

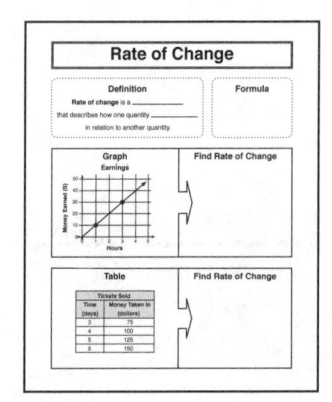

CD-405047 © Mark Twain Media, Inc., Publishers

Interactive Math Notebook: Grade 8 — Left-hand Page: Rate of Change

Rate of Change

Definition

Rate of change is a _____ that describes how one quantity _____ in relation to another quantity.

Formula

Graph

Earnings

(Graph showing Money Earned ($) vs. Hours, with points at (1, 10) and (3, 30))

Find Rate of Change

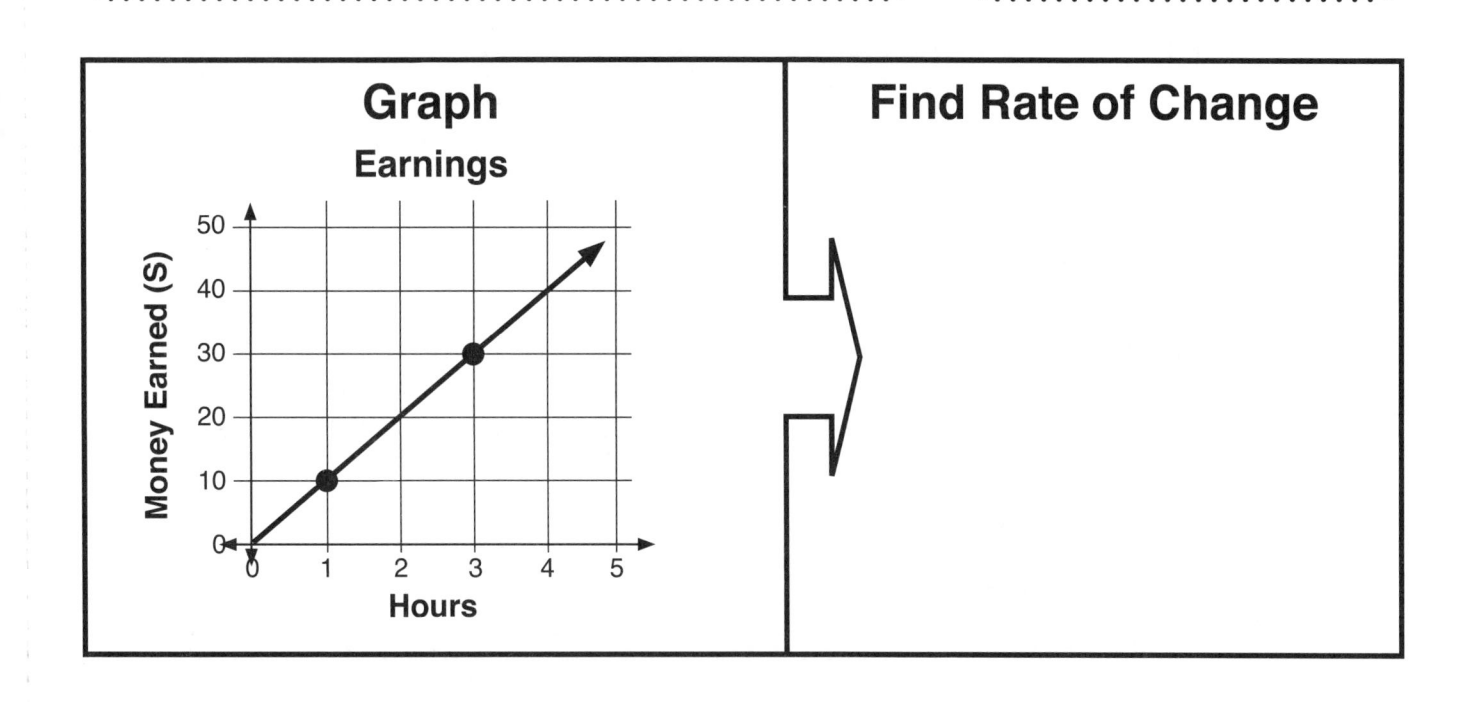

Table

Tickets Sold	
Time (days)	Money Taken In (dollars)
3	75
4	100
5	125
6	150

Find Rate of Change

CD-405047 © Mark Twain Media, Inc., Publishers

Interactive Math Notebook: Grade 8

Student Instructions: Linear & Nonlinear Functions

Student Instructions: Linear & Nonlinear Functions

Read the following information. Cut out the mini-lesson and attach it to the right-hand page of your interactive notebook. Use what you have learned to create the left-hand page.

Mini-Lesson

Linear & Nonlinear Functions

Functions can be classified in two different ways: linear and nonlinear. Graphs and tables are used to represent functions.

Linear functions have graphs that are straight lines.

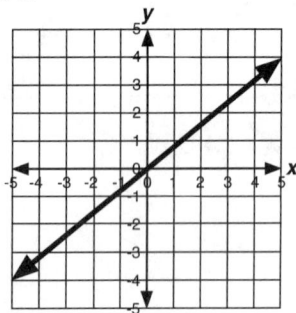

Nonlinear functions have graphs that are not straight lines.

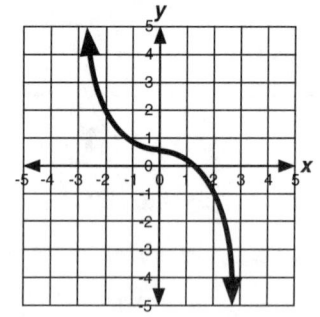

Table
The rates of change between any two data points is a constant. *y* increases or decreases at a constant rate, as *x* increases at a constant rate.

x	5	10	15	20
y	16	12	8	4

+5, +5, +5
−4, −4, −4

Table
The rates of change are not constant. *y* increases or decreases at different amounts each time, as *x* increases at a constant rate.

x	1	2	3	4
y	1	3	6	15

+1, +1, +1
+2, +3, +9

Descriptions used in word sentences include *per, each,* or *every.* A linear function has an equation that can be written in the form $y = mx + b$.

A nonlinear function has an equation that can be written in the form $y = x^2 + b$. Descriptions used in word sentences include *cubed, squared,* or *exponentially.*

Create Your Left-hand Notebook Page

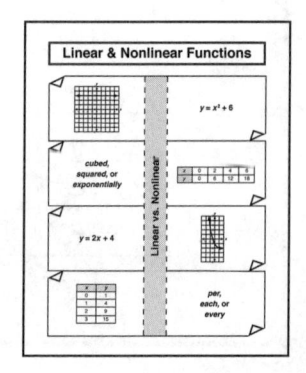

Step 1: Cut out the title and glue it to the top of the notebook page.
Step 2: Cut out the *Linear vs. Nonlinear* flap book. Cut on the solid lines to create eight flaps. Apply glue to the back of the gray center section and attach it below the title.
Step 3: Under each flap, identify the type of function represented.

CD-405047 © Mark Twain Media, Inc., Publishers

Linear & Nonlinear Functions

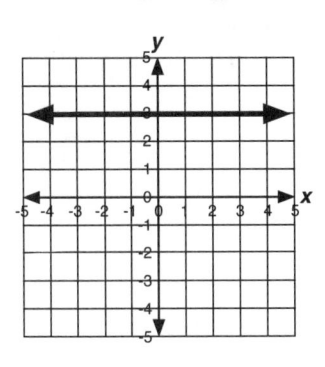

Linear vs. Nonlinear

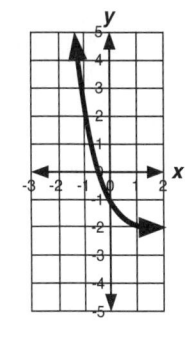

Linear	Nonlinear
(horizontal line graph)	$y = x^2 + 6$
cubed, *squared*, or *exponentially*	x: 0, 2, 4, 6 / y: 0, 6, 12, 18
$y = 2x + 4$	(decreasing curve graph)
x: 0,1,2,3 / y: 1,4,9,15	*per*, *each*, or *every*

Interactive Math Notebook: Grade 8 — Student Instructions: Translations on the Coordinate Plane

Student Instructions: Translations on the Coordinate Plane

Read the following information. Cut out the mini-lesson and attach it to the right-hand page of your interactive notebook. Use what you have learned to create the left-hand page.

Mini-Lesson

Translations on the Coordinate Plane

Transformation is a way to change the position of a figure. The original figure is called the **preimage**. The **image** is the position of the figure after a transformation. An arrow (→) is used to describe a transformation. The prime symbol (') is used to label the image (A').

Translation is one type of transformation. A **translation** slides a figure from one position to another without turning it. A coordinate plane is used to map the preimage and the image. Every point of the preimage is moved the same distance and in the same direction. The image and the preimage are congruent (have the same shape and size).

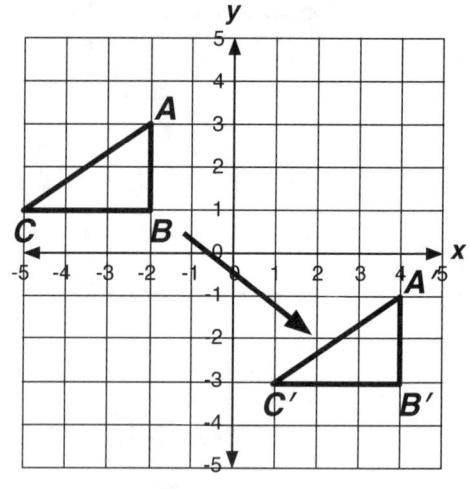

△ABC → △A'B'C'

Describing Translations
- Notation is used to describe translations, $(x, y) \rightarrow (x + a, y + b)$.
- Words such as "move 3 units (squares) right and 5 units down" on the coordinate plane are used to describe translations. When the movement is left, the value of *a* in the notation is negative. If the movement is down, then *b* is negative.

Using a Table
Triangle *ABC* above has vertices *A*(-2, 3), *B*(-2, 1) and *C*(-5, 1). The table to the right shows how to use notation to find the vertices of △*A'B'C'* after translation of 6 units right and 4 units down. Therefore, 6 was added to the *x*-coordinates and -4 was added to the *y*-coordinates.

Translation Notation $(x, y) \rightarrow (x + a, y + b)$		
Vertices of △ABC	$(x + 6, y + -4)$	**Vertices of △A'B'C'**
A(-2, 3)	(-2 + 6, -4 + 3)	A'(4, -1)
B(-2, 1)	(-2 + 6, -4 + 1)	B'(4, -3)
C(-5, 1)	(-5 + 6, -4 + 1)	C'(1, -3)

Create Your Left-hand Notebook Page

Step 1: Cut out the title and glue it to the top of the notebook page.
Step 2: Fill in the blanks on the *Definitions* piece. Cut out the piece. Apply glue to the back and attach it below the title.
Step 3: Complete the table on the *Translation Notation* piece. Find the vertices of △*A'B'C'* after a translation of 2 units left and 1 unit up. Cut out the table. Apply glue to the back and attach it below the title.
Step 4: Complete the graph on the *Translation* flap piece. Graph the image of △*A'B'C'* after a translation 2 units right and 5 units down. Under the flap, write the coordinates of its vertices.

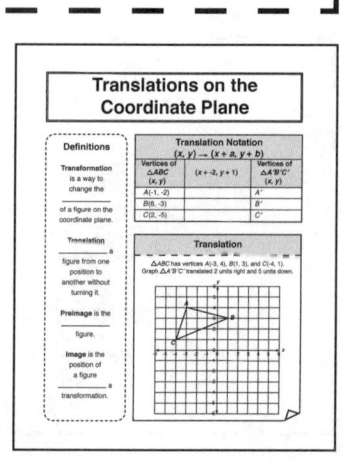

CD-405047 © Mark Twain Media, Inc., Publishers

Translations on the Coordinate Plane

Definitions

Transformation is a way to change the _____ of a figure on the coordinate plane.

Translation _____ a figure from one position to another without turning it.

Preimage is the _____ figure.

Image is the position of a figure _____ a transformation.

Translation Notation
$(x, y) \rightarrow (x + a, y + b)$

Vertices of △ABC (x, y)	(x + -2, y + 1)	Vertices of △A′B′C′ (x, y)
A(-1, -2)		A′
B(6, -3)		B′
C(2, -5)		C′

Translation

△ABC has vertices A(-3, 4), B(1, 3), and C(-4, 1). Graph △A′B′C′ translated 2 units right and 5 units down.

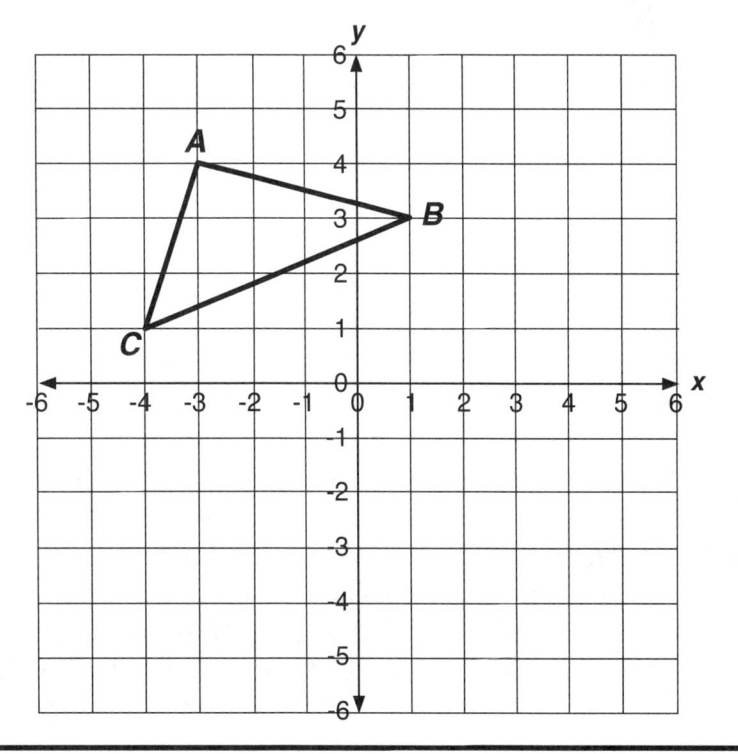

Interactive Math Notebook: Grade 8 — Student Instructions: Reflections on the Coordinate Plane

Student Instructions: Reflections on the Coordinate Plane

Read the following information. Cut out the mini-lesson and attach it to the right-hand page of your interactive notebook. Use what you have learned to create the left-hand page.

Mini-Lesson

Reflections on the Coordinate Plane

A **reflection** is a transformation representing a flip of a figure. The refection is a mirror image of the original figure. A reflection maps every point of a figure to an image across a fixed line. The fixed line is called the **line of reflection**. The image is **congruent** to the preimage (has the same shape and size). All points of the preimage and all points of the image are the same distance from the line of reflection.

Rules for Reflections on the Coordinate Plane

Reflection over *x*-axis	Reflection over *y*-axis
Rule: To reflect a figure over the *x*-axis, multiply the *y*-coordinates by -1.	**Rule:** To reflect a figure over the y-axis, multiply the *x*-coordinates by -1.
Notation: $(x, y) \longrightarrow (x, -y)$	**Notation:** $(x, y) \longrightarrow (-x, y)$
Example: Point A is 4 units above the *x*-axis. Point A′ is 4 units below the *x*-axis.	**Example:** Point A is 4 units to the left of the *x*-axis. Point A′ is 4 units to the right of the *x*-axis.
△**ABC** vertices: $A(-4, 4), B(-2, 1), C(-4, 1)$	△**ABC** vertices: $A(-4, 4), B(-2, 1), C(-4, 1)$
△**A′B′C′** vertices: $A'(-4,-4), B'(-2,-1), C'(-4,-1)$	△**A′B′C′** vertices: $A'(4, 4), B'(2, 1), C'(4, 1)$

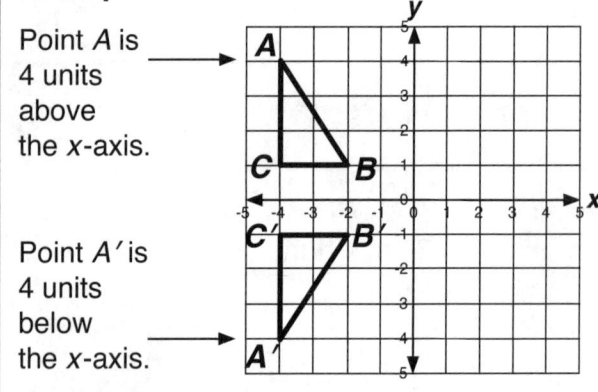

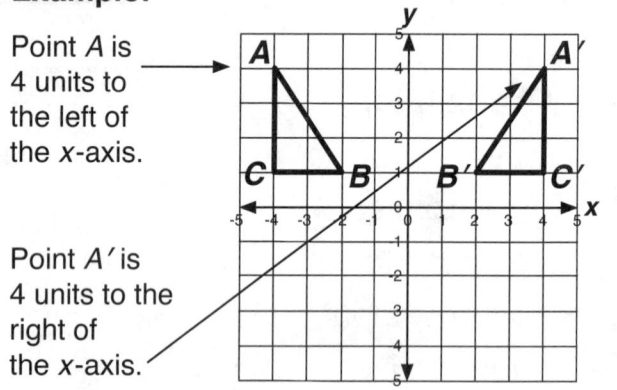

Create Your Left-hand Notebook Page

Step 1: Cut out the title and glue it to the top of the notebook page.

Step 2: On the *Reflection over x-axis* flap book, graph the reflected image over the *x*-axis. Cut out the flap book. Cut on the solid lines to create three flaps. Apply glue to the back of the left-hand section of the flap book and attach it below the title. Under each flap, write the correct information for the graph.

Step 3: On the *Reflection over y-axis* flap book, graph the reflected image over the *y*-axis. Cut out the flap book. Cut on the solid lines to create three flaps. Apply glue to the back of the left-hand section of the flap book and attach it at the bottom of the page. Under each flap, write the correct information for the graph.

CD-405047 © Mark Twain Media, Inc., Publishers

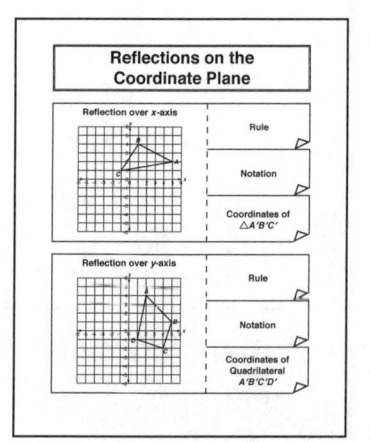

Interactive Math Notebook: Grade 8 Left-hand Page: Reflections on the Coordinate Plane

Reflections on the Coordinate Plane

Reflection over *x*-axis

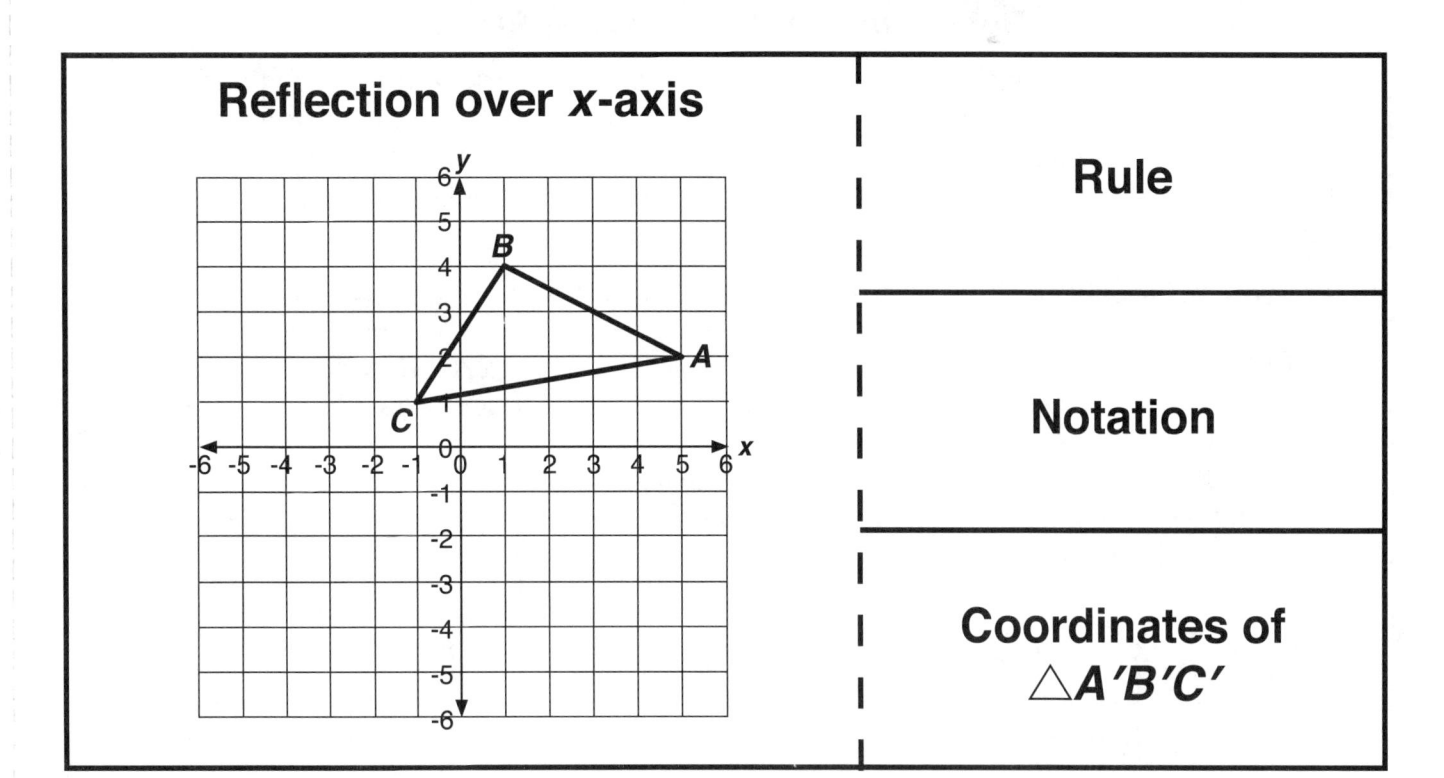

	Rule
	Notation
	Coordinates of △A′B′C′

Reflection over *y*-axis

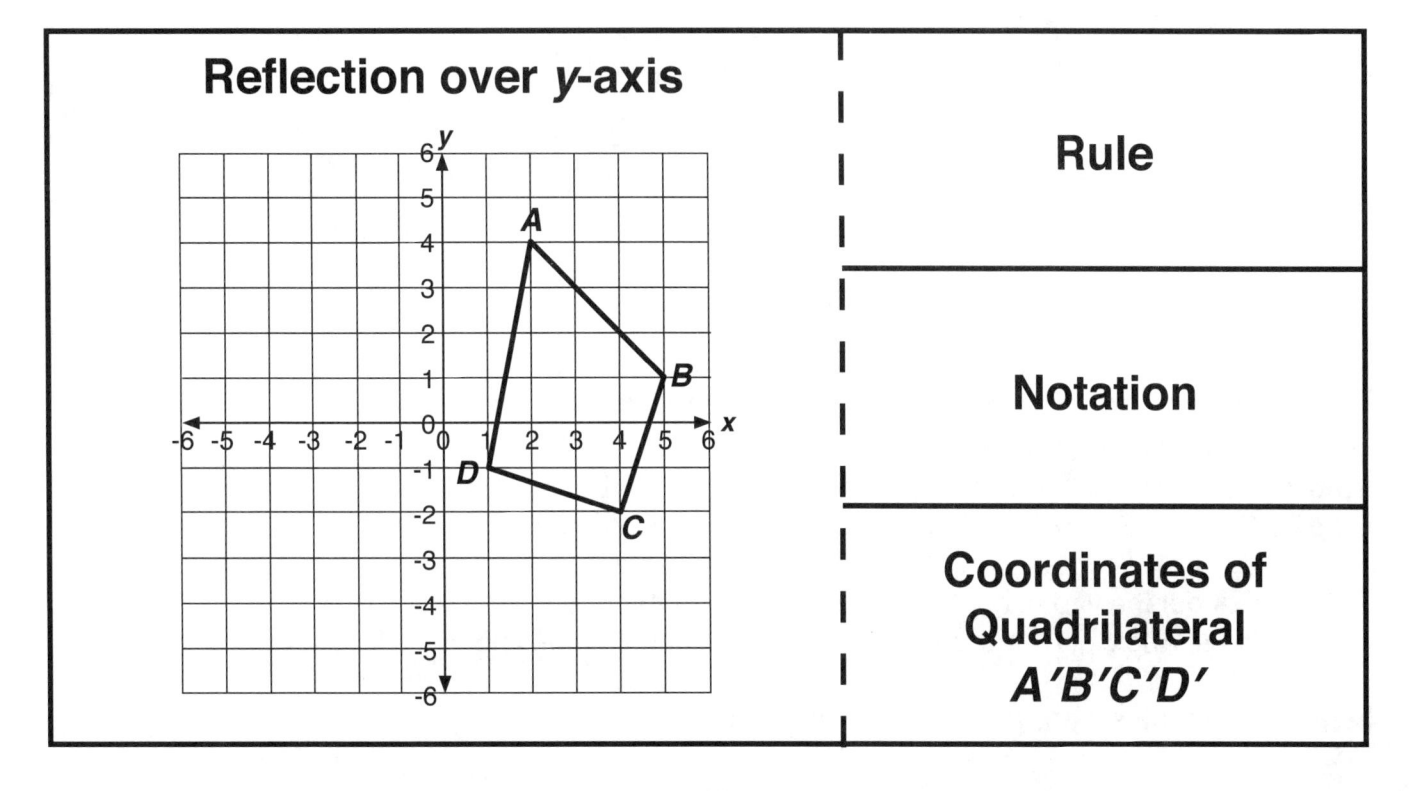

	Rule
	Notation
	Coordinates of Quadrilateral A′B′C′D′

Interactive Math Notebook: Grade 8 — Student Instructions: Rotations on the Coordinate Plane

Student Instructions: Rotations on the Coordinate Plane

Read the following information. Cut out the mini-lesson and attach it to the right-hand page of your interactive notebook. Use what you have learned to create the left-hand page.

Mini-Lesson

Rotations on the Coordinate Plane

A **rotation** is a transformation that represents the rotation (turn) of a figure around a fixed point. The **center of rotation** or origin (0) is the fixed point. The image is **congruent** to the preimage (has the same shape and size) but may be turned in a different direction. All points of the preimage and all points of the image are the same distance from the center of rotation. Rotations can be clockwise ↻ or counterclockwise ↺.

Examples of Clockwise Rotations on the Coordinate Plane

90° Rotation	180° Rotation	270° Rotation
Notation: $(x, y) \longrightarrow (y, -x)$	**Notation:** $(x, y) \longrightarrow (-x, -y)$	**Notation:** $(x, y) \longrightarrow (-y, x)$
Rule: Change signs of x-value. Switch x- and y-coordinates.	**Rule:** Change sign of x- and y-values.	**Rule:** Change sign of y-value. Switch x- and y-coordinates.
$(-4, 1) \longrightarrow (4, 1) \longrightarrow (1, 4)$	$(-4, 1) \longrightarrow (4, -1)$	$(-4, 1) \longrightarrow (-4, -1) \longrightarrow (-1, -4)$

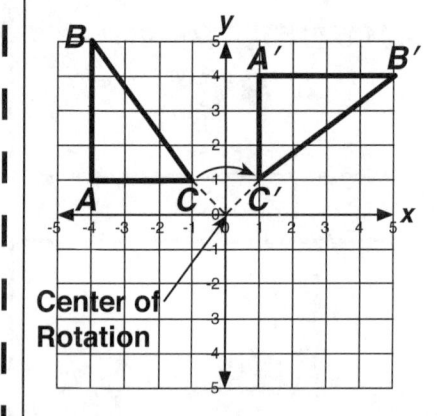

Center of Rotation

△ABC Vertices:
A(-4, 1), B(-4, 5), C(-1, 1)
△A'B'C' Vertices:
A'(1, 4), B'(5, 4), C'(1, 1)

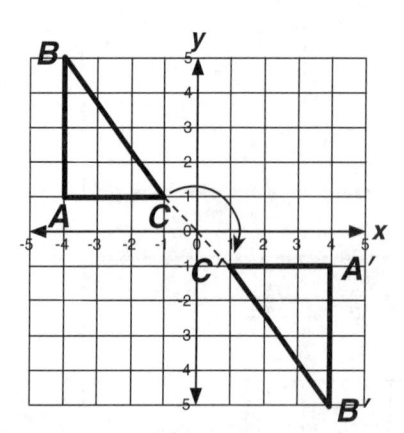

△ABC Vertices:
A(-4, 1), B(-4, 5), C(-1, 1)
△A'B'C' Vertices:
A'(4, -1), B'(4, -5), C'(1, -1)

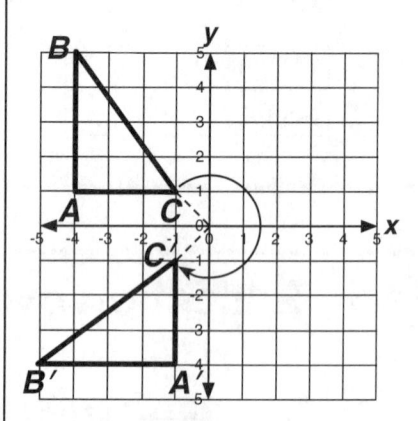

△ABC Vertices:
A(-4, 1), B(-4, 5), C(-1, 1)
△A'B'C' Vertices:
A'(-1, -4), B'(-5, -4), C'(-1, -1)

Your Left-hand Notebook Page

Step 1: Cut out the title and glue it to the top of the notebook page.
Step 2: Graph the △ABC on the *Triangle ABC* flap book after a clockwise rotation of 90°, 180°, and 270° about the origin. Cut out the flap book. Cut on the solid lines to create three flaps. Apply glue to the top section and attach it below the title.
Step 3: Under each flap, write the coordinates of the vertices for △A'B'C'.

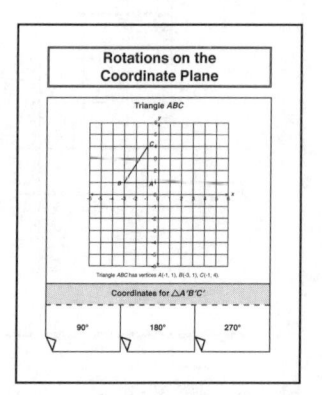

CD-405047 © Mark Twain Media, Inc., Publishers   44

Rotations on the Coordinate Plane

Triangle ABC

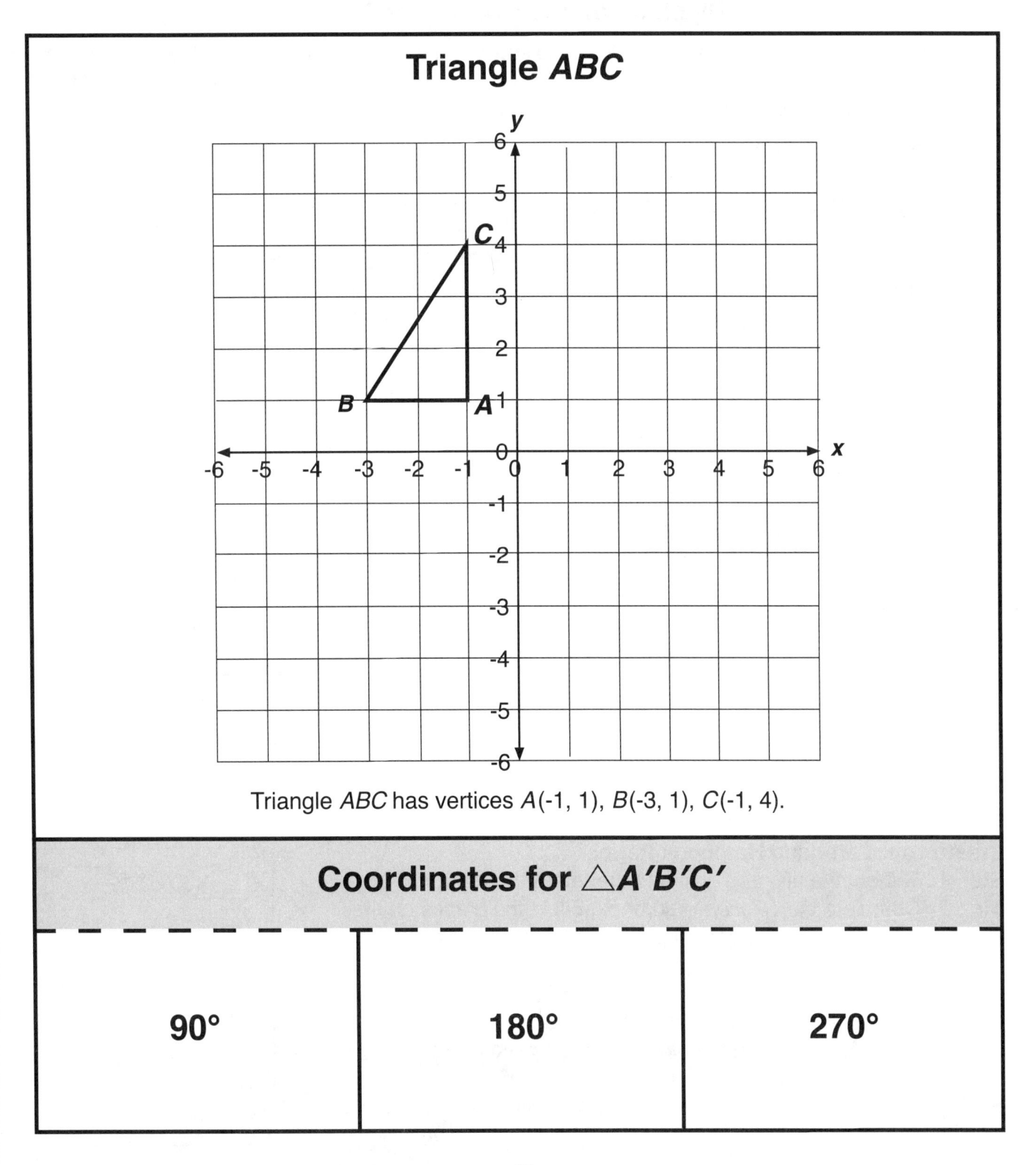

Triangle ABC has vertices A(-1, 1), B(-3, 1), C(-1, 4).

Coordinates for △A'B'C'

90°	180°	270°

Interactive Math Notebook: Grade 8   Student Instructions: Dilations on the Coordinate Plane

Student Instructions: Dilations on the Coordinate Plane

Read the following information. Cut out the mini-lesson and attach it to the right-hand page of your interactive notebook. Use what you have learned to create the left-hand page.

Mini-Lesson

Dilations on the Coordinate Plane

Dilation is a transformation that changes the size of a figure. Dilation includes the scale factor and the center of the dilation. The **scale factor** refers to the amount of change in the size of the figure. The **center of dilation** is a fixed point on the coordinate plane, usually the origin, (0, 0).

Two Types of Dilations

Enlargement: scale factor (k) is > 1 or $k > 1$. **Rule:** Each coordinate of the preimage is multiplied by the scale factor k to find the coordinates of the image. **Notation:** $(x, y) \rightarrow (kx, ky)$	**Reduction:** scale factor (k) is between 0 and 1 or $0 < k < 1$. **Rule:** Each coordinate of the preimage is multiplied by the scale factor k to find the coordinates of the image. **Notation:** $(x, y) \rightarrow (kx, ky)$
Scale factor of 3: $(x, y) \rightarrow (3x, 3y)$ $A(1, 1) \rightarrow (3 \cdot 1, 3 \cdot 1) \rightarrow A'(3, 3)$ $B(2, 2) \rightarrow (3 \cdot 2, 3 \cdot 2) \rightarrow B'(6, 6)$ $C(3, 1) \rightarrow (3 \cdot 3, 3 \cdot 1) \rightarrow C'(9, 3)$	**Scale factor of $\frac{1}{2}$:** $(x, y) \rightarrow (\frac{1}{2}x, \frac{1}{2}y)$ $A(2, 2) \rightarrow (\frac{1}{2} \cdot 2, \frac{1}{2} \cdot 2) \rightarrow A'(1, 1)$ $B(2, 8) \rightarrow (\frac{1}{2} \cdot 2, \frac{1}{2} \cdot 8) \rightarrow B'(1, 4)$ $C(8, 2) \rightarrow (\frac{1}{2} \cdot 8, \frac{1}{2} \cdot 2) \rightarrow C'(4, 1)$

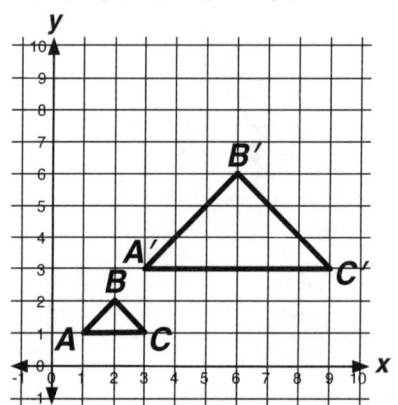

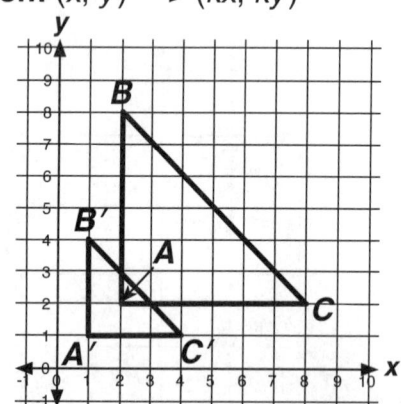

Create Your Left-hand Notebook Page

Step 1: Cut out the title and glue it to the top of the notebook page.

Step 2: Complete the *Dilations* flap book. Fill in the blanks on the gray tab. Find the coordinates of the vertices of each figure after a dilation with the given scale factor. Fill in the blanks with your answers. Then graph the dilation.

Step 3: Cut out the flap book. Cut on the solid line to create two flaps. Apply glue to the back of the gray tab and attach it below the title.

Step 4: Under each flap, write the rule and notation of the dilation.

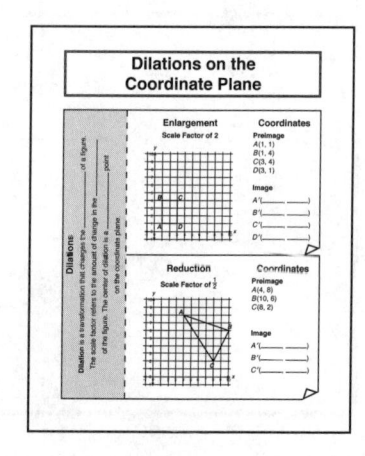

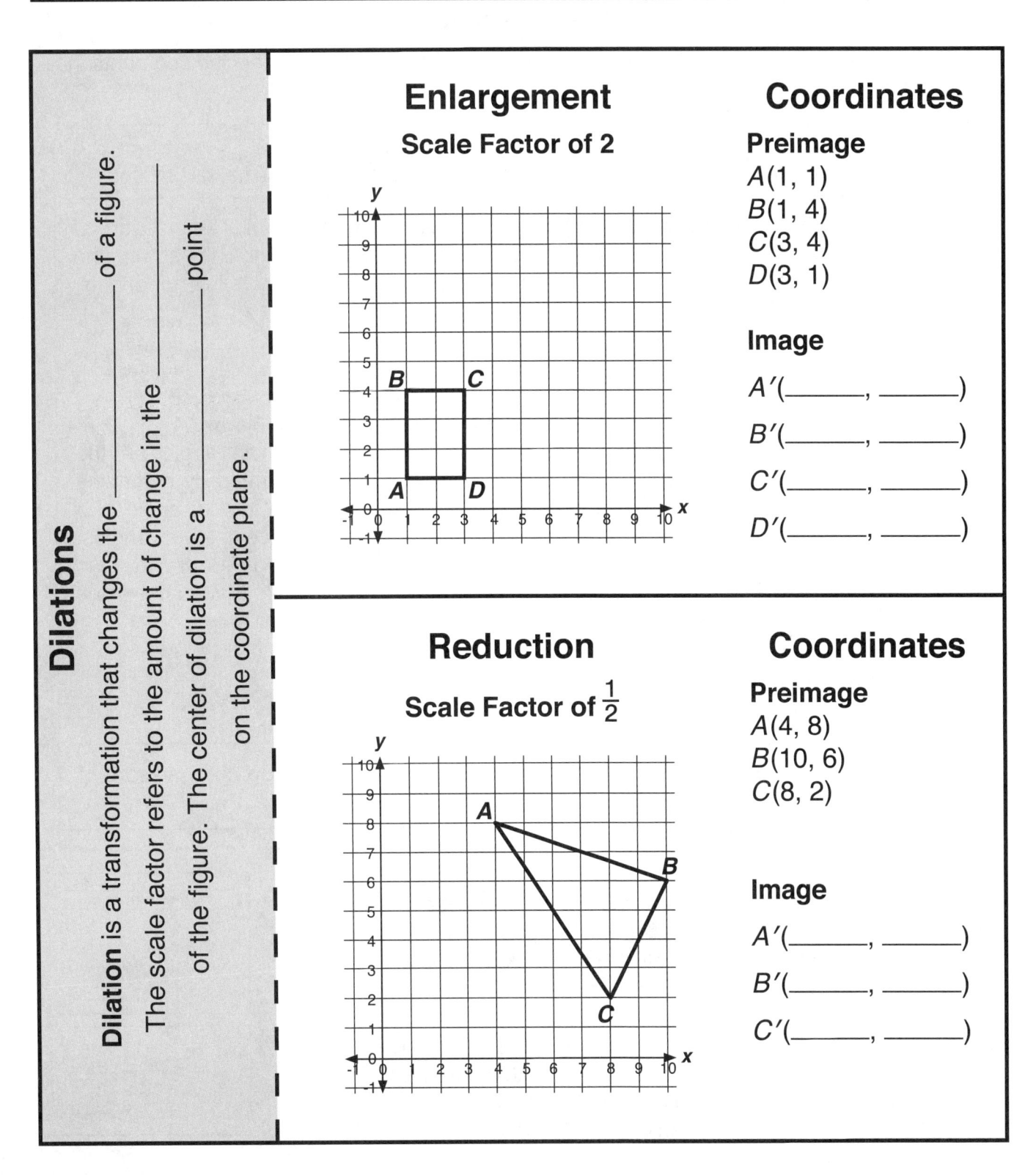

Interactive Math Notebook: Grade 8 Left-hand Page: Dilations on the Coordinate Plane

Dilations on the Coordinate Plane

Dilations

Dilation is a transformation that changes the _____ of a figure. The scale factor refers to the amount of change in the _____ of the figure. The center of dilation is a _____ point on the coordinate plane.

Enlargement
Scale Factor of 2

Coordinates
Preimage
A(1, 1)
B(1, 4)
C(3, 4)
D(3, 1)

Image
A'(____, ____)
B'(____, ____)
C'(____, ____)
D'(____, ____)

Reduction
Scale Factor of $\frac{1}{2}$

Coordinates
Preimage
A(4, 8)
B(10, 6)
C(8, 2)

Image
A'(____, ____)
B'(____, ____)
C'(____, ____)

Interactive Math Notebook: Grade 8 Student Instructions: Angles of Triangles

Student Instructions: Angles of Triangles

Read the following information. Cut out the mini-lesson and attach it to the right-hand page of your interactive notebook. Use what you have learned to create the left-hand page.

Mini-Lesson

Angles of Triangles

A **triangle** is a two-dimensional, closed figure that is formed by joining three line segments that intersect only at their endpoints or **vertices**.

Triangle Angle Theorems

A **theorem** is a statement that can be proven to be true using mathemaical operations.

Interior Angle Theorem: The sum of the measure of the interior angles is always 180°.

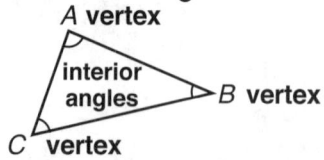

Formula: $\angle A + \angle B + \angle C = 180°$

An **interior angle** is an angle on the inside of a triangle. The symbol for angle is $\angle$. The correct way to name an angle is either to write angle ABC is $\angle ABC$, $\angle CBA$, or $\angle B$. The middle letter of the three is always the vertex.

Missing Angle
Find the value of x.
$x + 110 + 30 = 180$
$x + 140 = 180$
$-140 = -140$
$x = 40$

The value of x is 40. So, the measure of the missing angle is 40°.

Exterior Angle Theorem: The measure of an exterior angle is equal to the sum of the measures of its two remote interior angles.

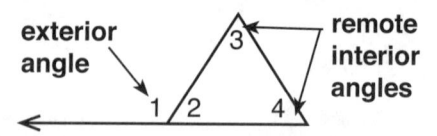

Formula: $m\angle 1 = m\angle 3 + m\angle 4$

An **exterior angle** is an angle on the outside of a triangle formed by extending one of the sides. Each interior angle of a triangle has two remote interior angles. The **remote interior angles** are the two angles inside the triangle that do not share a vertex with the exterior angle.

Missing Angle
Find the value of x.
$x = 63 + 86$
$x = 149$

The value of x is 149. So, the measure of the missing angle is 149°.

Create Your Left-hand Notebook Page
Step 1: Cut out the title and glue it to the top of the notebook page.
Step 2: Cut out the *Interior Angles* flap book. Cut on the solid lines to create four flaps. Apply glue to the back of the gray center section and attach it below the title. Under each flap, write the correct information.
Step 3: Cut out the *Exterior Angles* flap book. Cut on the solid lines to create four flaps. Apply glue to the back of the gray center section and attach it at the bottom of the page. Under each flap, write the correct information.

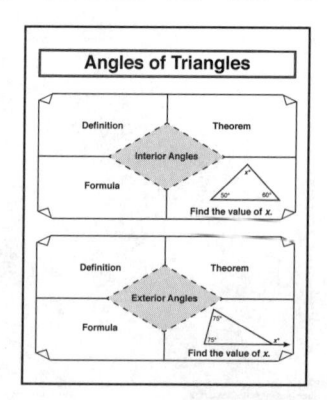

CD-405047 © Mark Twain Media, Inc., Publishers

Angles of Triangles

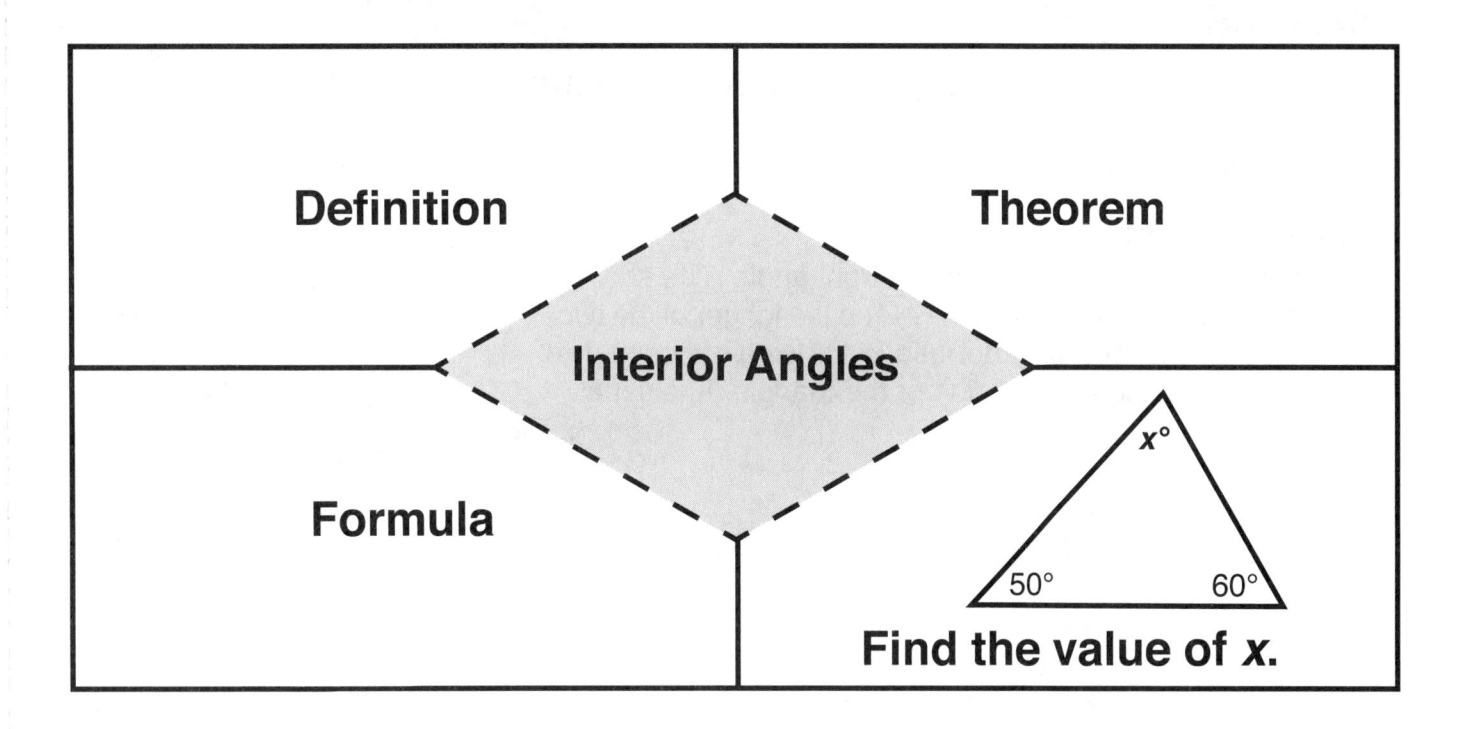

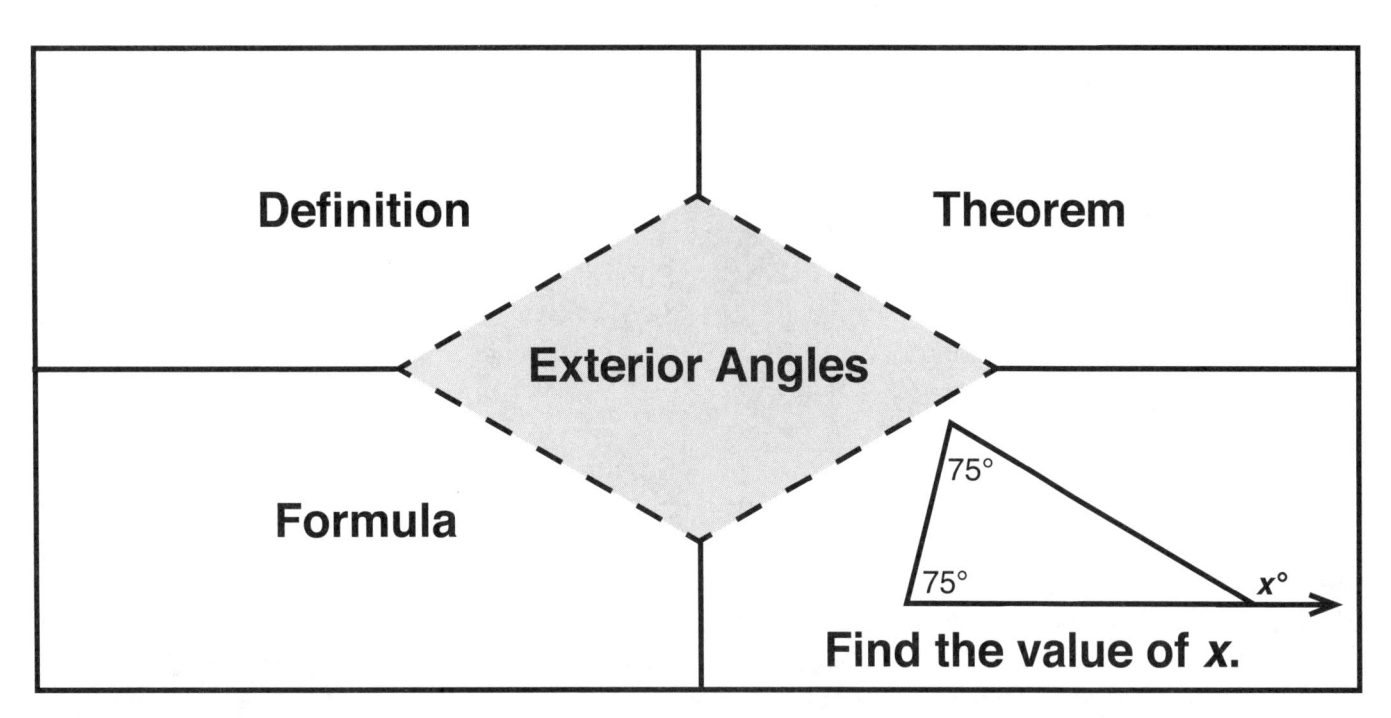

Definition

Theorem

Interior Angles

Formula

Find the value of *x*.
(Triangle with angles x°, 50°, 60°)

Definition

Theorem

Exterior Angles

Formula

Find the value of *x*.
(Triangle with angles 75°, 75°, and exterior angle x°)

Student Instructions: The Pythagorean Theorem

Read the following information. Cut out the mini-lesson and attach it to the right-hand page of your interactive notebook. Use what you have learned to create the left-hand page.

Mini-Lesson

The Pythagorean Theorem

A **right triangle** is a triangle with one right angle, also called a 90-degree angle.

Parts of a Right Triangle
The **legs** are the sides that form the right angle. The shorter of the two sides is usually labeled **a**, and the longer of the two legs is usually **b**. The **hypotenuse** is the side opposite the right angle. It is the longest side of the triangle. It is usually labeled **c**.

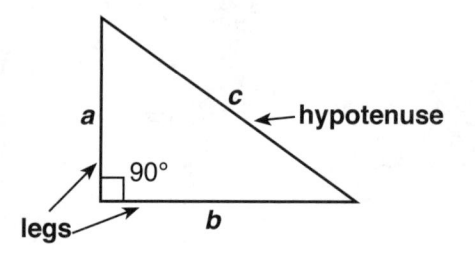

Pythagorean Theorem
You can use the Pythagorean Theorem to find the unknown length of one side of a right triangle.

Pythagorean Theorem: given any right triangle, the square of the length of the longest side will equal the sum of the squares of the lengths of the two shorter sides.	**Formula:** $a^2 + b^2 = c^2$

Example 1:
Find the missing length.
$a^2 + b^2 = c^2$
$3^2 + 4^2 = c^2$
$9 + 16 = c^2$
$25 = c^2$
$\sqrt{25} = c$
$5 = c$
So, the hypotenuse is 5 ft. long.

Example 2:
Find the missing length.
$a^2 + b^2 = c^2$
$a^2 + 12^2 = 15^2$
$a^2 + 144 = 225$

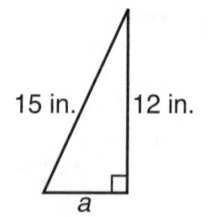

Subtract 144 from each side to get:
$144 - 144 + a^2 = 225 - 144$
$a^2 = 81$
$a = \sqrt{81}$
$a = 9$
So, the length of side *a* is 9 inches.

Create Your Left-hand Notebook Page
Step 1: Cut out the title and glue it to the top of the notebook page.
Step 2: On the front of the *Definitions* puzzle piece, write the meaning below each of the three vocabulary words. Cut out the piece. Apply glue to the back and attach it below the title.
Step 3: On the front of the *Find Missing Length* puzzle pieces, use the Pythagorean Theorem formula to find the missing length of each right triangle. Cut out the piece. Apply glue to the back and attach it at the bottom of the page.

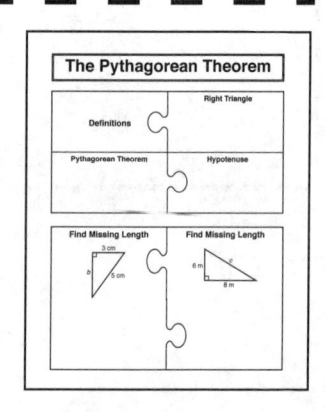

The Pythagorean Theorem

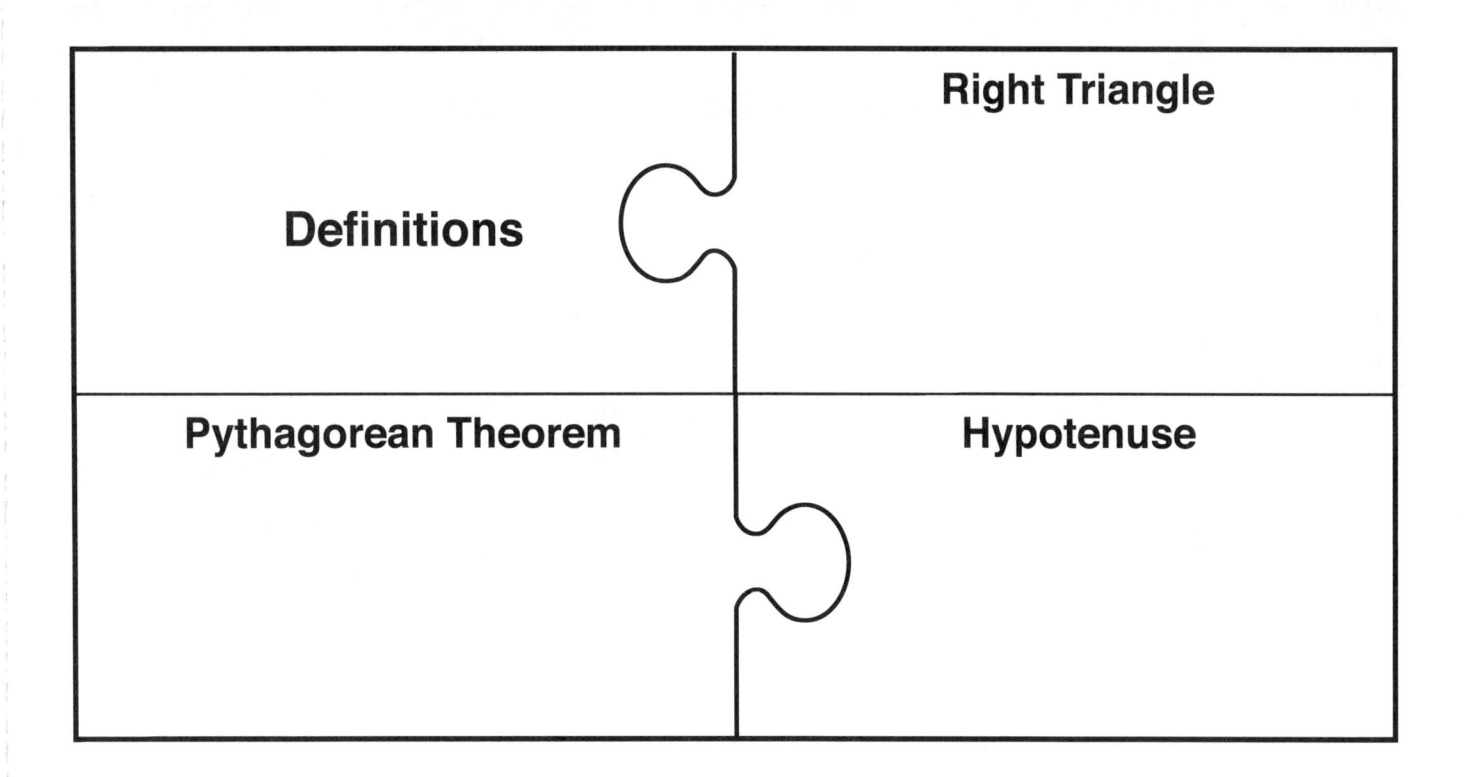

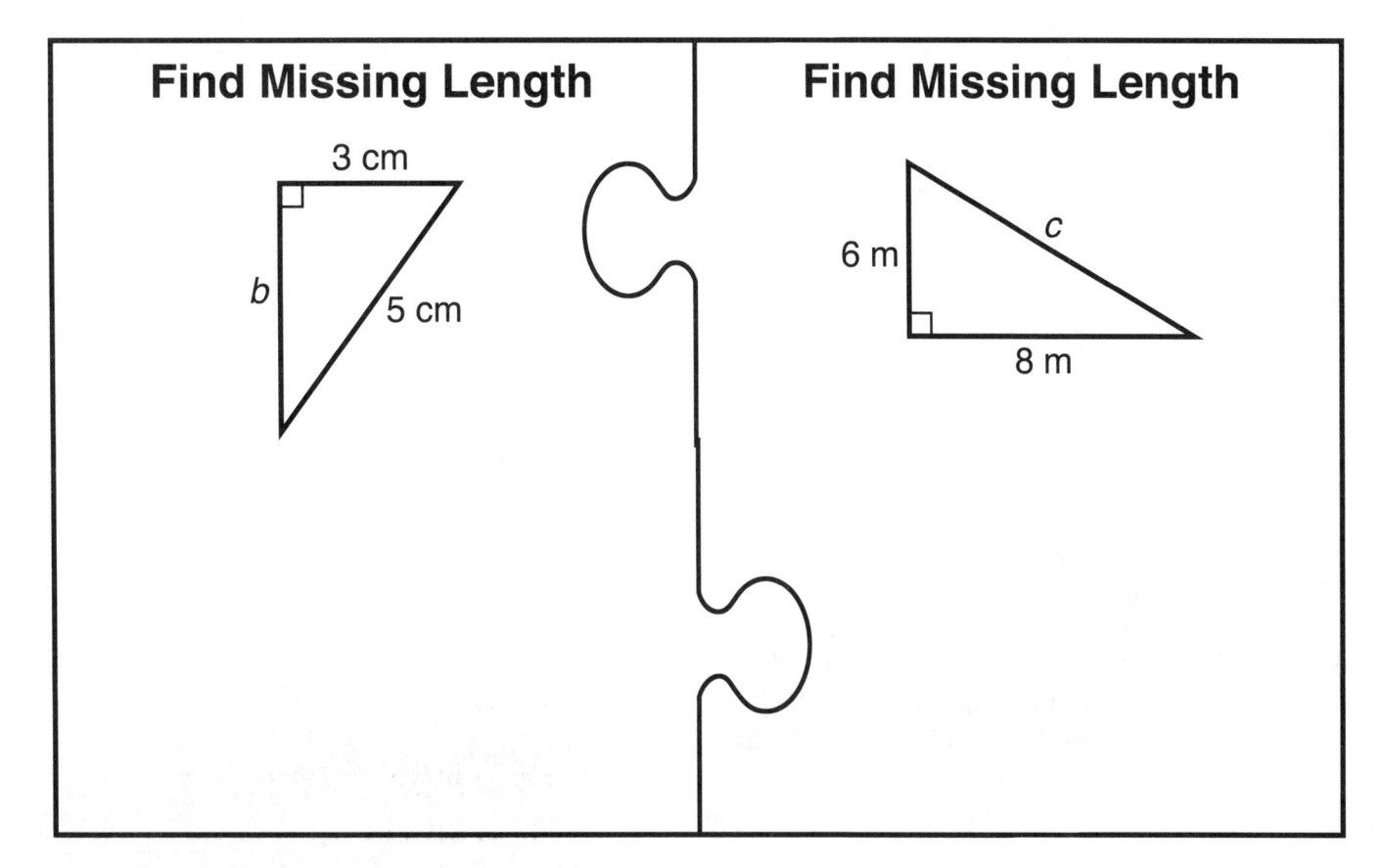

Definitions	Right Triangle
Pythagorean Theorem	Hypotenuse

Find Missing Length

3 cm
b
5 cm

Find Missing Length

6 m
c
8 m

Interactive Math Notebook: Grade 8   Student Instructions: Distance on the Coordinate Plane

Student Instructions: Distance on the Coordinate Plane

Read the following information. Cut out the mini-lesson and attach it to the right-hand page of your interactive notebook. Use what you have learned to create the left-hand page.

Mini-Lesson

Distance on the Coordinate Plane

The distance between two points on a coordinate plane can be found using the Pythagorean Theorem. **Formula:** $a^2 + b^2 = c^2$

Find the Distance Between Two Points

Step 1: Graph the ordered pairs.
 A (1, 2)
 B (5, 5)
Connect the two points with a line.

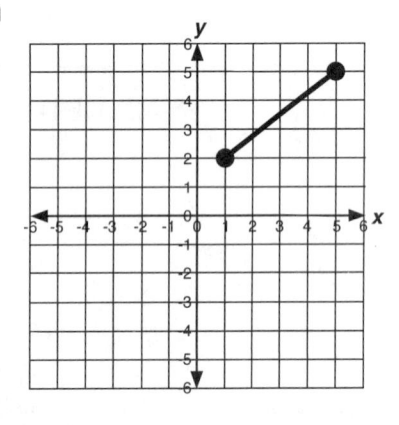

Step 2: Draw a vertical and horizontal line to form the legs of the right triangle with *c* as the hypotenuse (longest side).

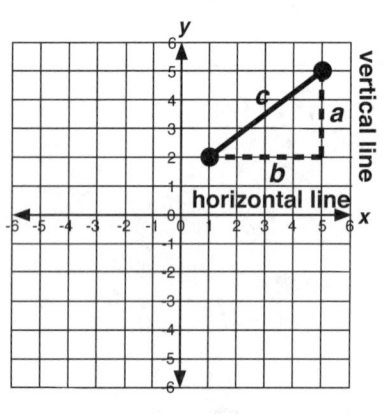

Step 3: Measure the distance of the vertical and horizontal lines to find the length of the two legs (short sides) of the triangle.

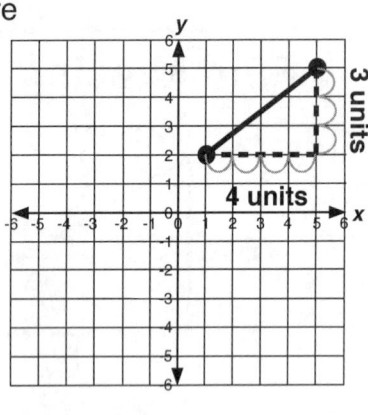

Step 4: Now that we know the length of *a* and *b*, we can plug those values into the formula to find the length of side *c*.

$$a^2 + b^2 = c^2$$
$$3^2 + 4^2 = c^2$$
$$9 + 16 = c^2$$
$$25 = c^2$$
$$\sqrt{25} = c$$
$$5 = c$$

So, the distance is 5 units.

Create Your Left-hand Notebook Page

Step 1: Cut out the title and glue it to the top of the notebook page.
Step 2: Fill in the blanks on the *Pythagorean Theorem* piece. Cut out the piece. Apply glue to the back and attach it below the title.
Step 3: Follow steps 1 to 3 for finding the distance between two points to complete the graph on the *Coordinate Plane* piece. Now that you know the length of *a* and *b*, plug those values into the formula and find the length of side *c*. Cut out the piece. Apply glue to the back and attach it at the bottom of the page.

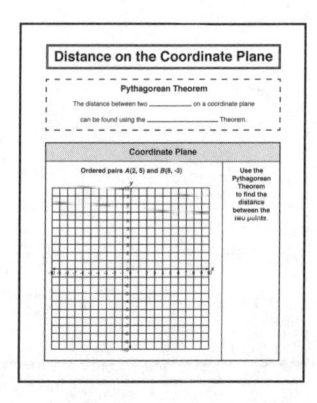

Distance on the Coordinate Plane

Pythagorean Theorem

The distance between two _____ on a coordinate plane

can be found using the _____ Theorem.

Coordinate Plane

Ordered pairs A(2, 5) and B(8, -3)

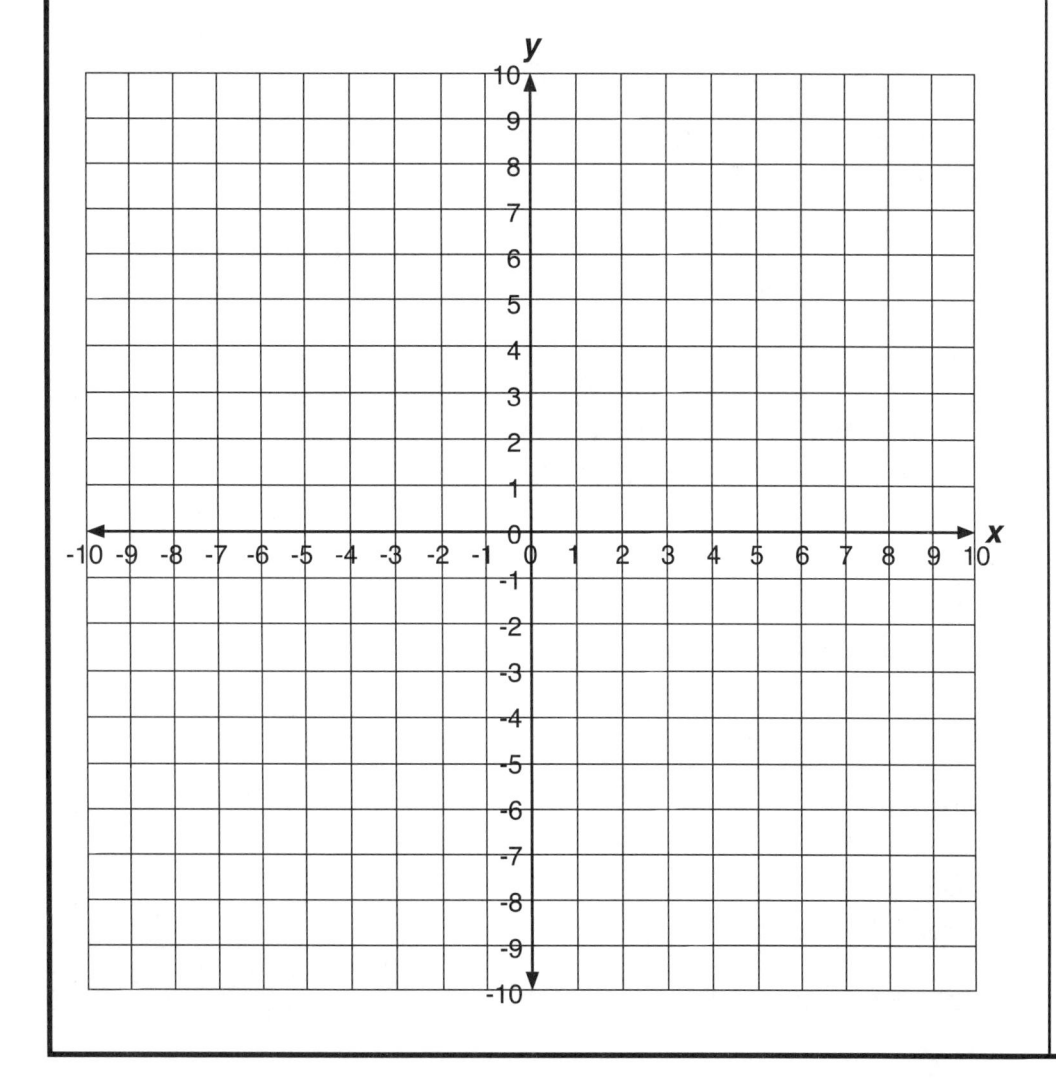

Use the Pythagorean Theorem to find the distance between the two points.

Interactive Math Notebook: Grade 8   Student Instructions: Volume of Cones, Cylinders, & Spheres

Student Instructions: Volume of Cones, Cylinders, & Spheres

Read the following information. Cut out the mini-lesson and attach it to the right-hand page of your interactive notebook. Use what you have learned to create the left-hand page.

Mini-Lesson

Volume of Cones, Cylinders, & Spheres

Volume is the measure of the amount of space inside of a figure. Volume is measured in **cubic units** (cu) such as cm^3. **Pi** (π) is used to figure the volume of cones, cylinders, and spheres. Whenever 3.14 is used for π, you are finding the approximate equal ($\approx$) value.

Strategy for Finding Volume of Cones

	Identify Radius of Base	Find Area of Base (*B*)	Identify Height	Find Volume
5 ft. / 2 ft. (cone)	2 ft.	$A = \pi r^2$ $A = 3.14 \cdot 2^2$ $A = 3.14 \cdot 4$ $A = 12.56$ ft.^{2}	5 ft.	$V = \frac{1}{3}Bh$ $V = \frac{12.56 \cdot 5}{3}$ $V = \frac{62.8}{3}$ $V \approx 20.93$ ft.^{3}

Strategy for Finding Volume of Cylinders

	Identify Radius of Base	Find Area of Base (*B*)	Identify Height	Find Volume
3 m / 6 m (cylinder)	3 m	$A = \pi r^2$ $A = 3.14 \cdot 3^2$ $A = 3.14 \cdot 9$ $A = 28.26$ m^2	6 m	$V = Bh$ $V = 28.26 \cdot 6$ $V \approx 169.6$ m^3

Strategy for Finding Volume of Spheres

	Identify Radius	Find Value of Radius Cubed	Calculate Pi Times Radius Cubed	Find Volume
8 m (sphere)	8 m	$V = \frac{4}{3}\pi r^3$ $V = \frac{4}{3}\pi 8^3$ $V = \frac{4}{3}(\pi \cdot 512)$	$V = \frac{4}{3}\pi r^3$ $V = \frac{4}{3}(3.14 \cdot 512)$ $V = \frac{4}{3}(1607.68)$	$V = \frac{4}{3}\pi r^3$ $V = \frac{4}{3}\left(\frac{1607.68}{1}\right)$ $V = \frac{6430.72}{3}$ $V = 2143.57333$ $V \approx 2143.57$ m^3

Create Your Left-hand Notebook Page

Step 1: Cut out the title and glue it to the top of the notebook page.

Step 2: Complete the *Cone, Cylinder,* and *Sphere* pieces. Use 3.14 for π and round your answers to the nearest tenth. Show your work.

Step 3: Cut out the pieces. Apply glue to the backs and attach them below the title.

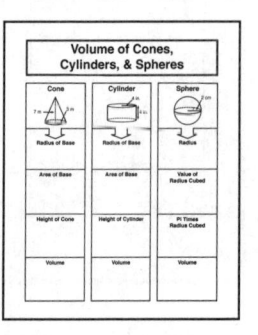

CD-405047 © Mark Twain Media, Inc., Publishers

Volume of Cones, Cylinders, & Spheres

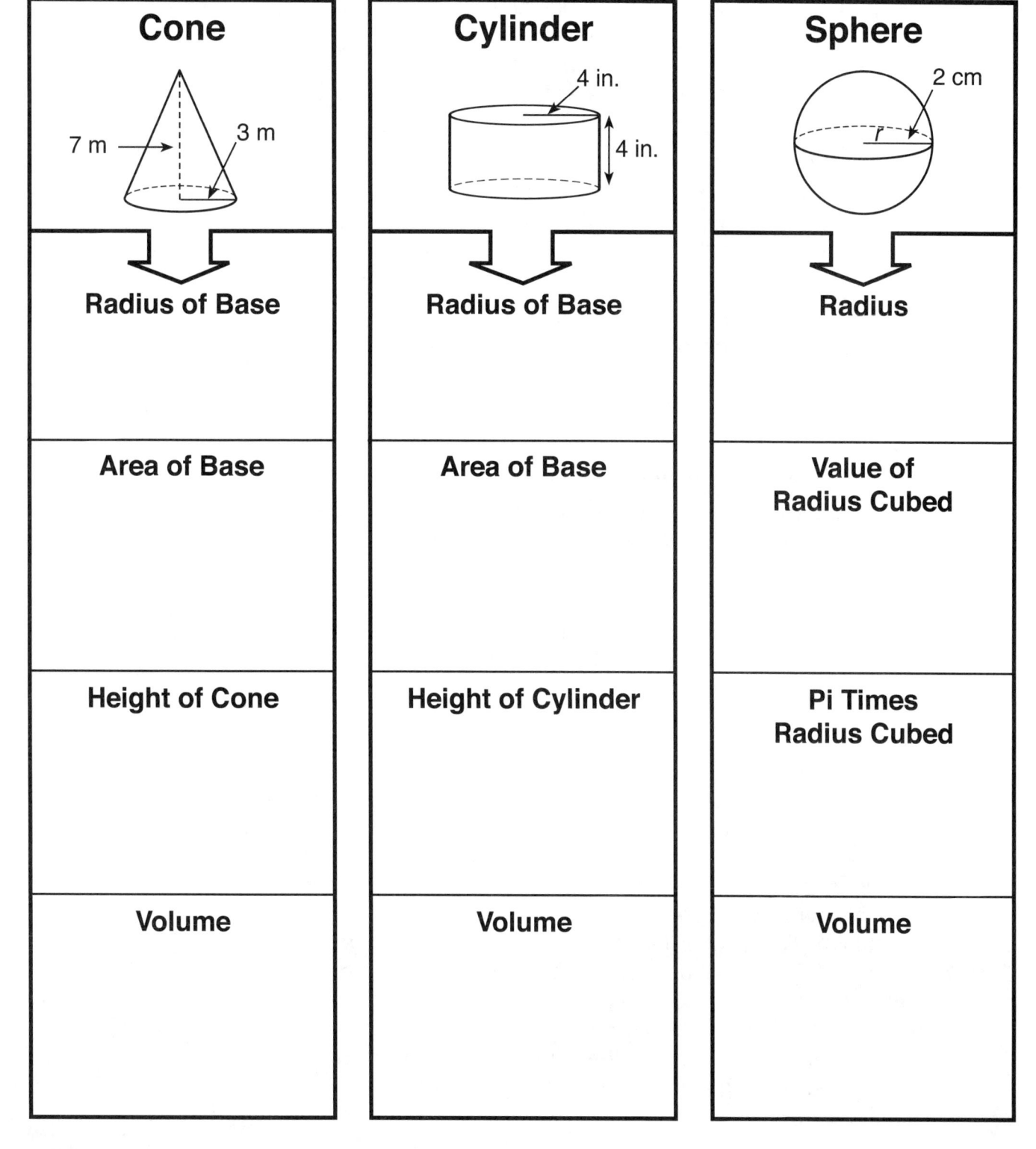

Cone	Cylinder	Sphere
7 m, 3 m	4 in., 4 in.	2 cm
Radius of Base	Radius of Base	Radius
Area of Base	Area of Base	Value of Radius Cubed
Height of Cone	Height of Cylinder	Pi Times Radius Cubed
Volume	Volume	Volume

Student Instructions: Scatter Plots

Read the following information. Cut out the mini-lesson and attach it to the right-hand page of your interactive notebook. Use what you have learned to create the left-hand page.

Mini-Lesson

Scatter Plots

A **scatter plot** is a graph of plotted points on a coordinate plane. The graph shows an association (relationship) between **bivariate data** or data with two variables, the *x* and *y* variables.

The plotted points often form a pattern. The pattern is used to describe the association between the *x* and *y* variables. The pattern is categorized as either **linear** (straight-line) or **nonlinear**.

Associations

Linear — Line of best fit. Plotted data points form a straight-line pattern or lie close to a straight line.

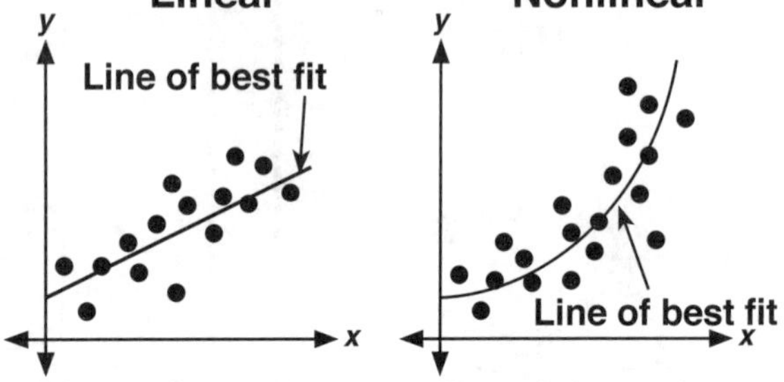

Nonlinear — Line of best fit. Plotted data points form a curved pattern.

In a linear association, the **line of best fit** is a straight line that best represents the plotted data. This line may pass through some of the points, none of the points, or all the points.

There are three types of linear associations: **positive association**, **negative association**, and **no association**.

Example: Association of Temperature and Sales

Positive Association
As *x* increases, *y* increases

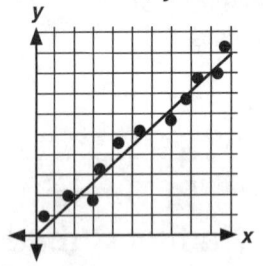

Negative Association
As *x* increases, *y* decreases

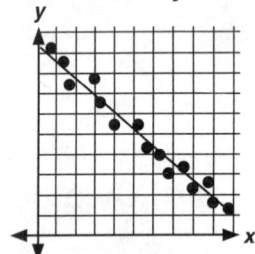

No Association
No obvious (clear) pattern

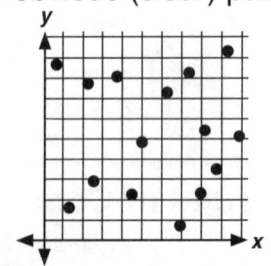

Interpret Scatter Plot:
As temperature (*x*) increased, soft drink sales (*y*) increased.

Interpret Scatter Plot:
As temperature (*x*) increased, coffee sales (*y*) decreased.

Interpret Scatter Plot:
Temperature had no obvious effect on ice cream sales.

Create Your Left-hand Notebook Page
Step 1: Cut out the title and glue it to the top of the notebook page.
Step 2: Cut out the *Type of Association* flap book. Cut on the solid lines to create three flaps. Apply glue to the back of the gray tab and attach it below the title.
Step 3: In each *Association* box, write the name of the association represented by the graph. Under each flap, interpret the scatter plot.

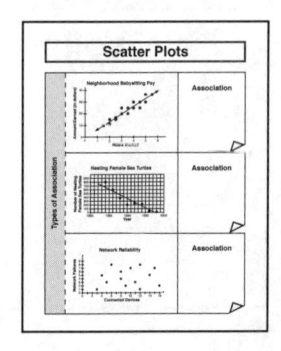

Scatter Plots

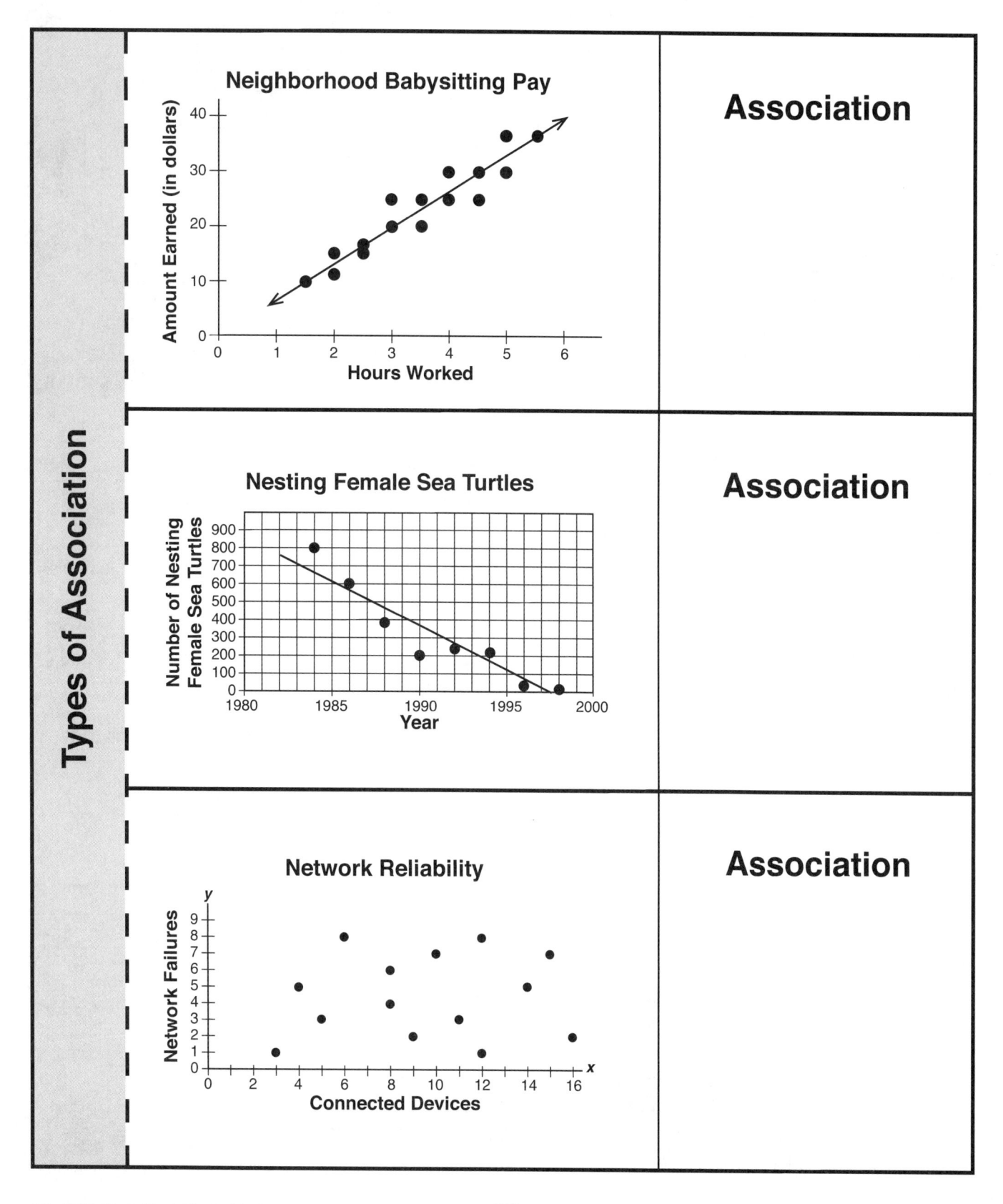

Types of Association

Neighborhood Babysitting Pay

Association

Nesting Female Sea Turtles

Association

Network Reliability

Association

Interactive Math Notebook: Grade 8   Student Instructions: Two-Way Tables

Student Instructions: Two-Way Tables

Read the following information. Cut out the mini-lesson and attach it to the right-hand page of your interactive notebook. Use what you have learned to create the left-hand page.

Mini-Lesson

Two-Way Tables

A **two-way table** is a visual presentation of the possible relationships between two different sets of **categorical data** (data placed into groups).

	Passed Test	Failed Test	Totals
Studied for Test	50	1	51
Did Not Study for Test	5	10	15
Totals	55	11	66

(Row Totals on the right; Column Totals on the bottom)

Parts of a Two-Way Table
Two-way tables are used to study data collected from surveys. One category of data is represented by rows, and the other is represented by columns. Each cell tells the frequency or count for the category. The totals of each row appear at the right, and the totals of each column appear at the bottom. The sum of the row totals equals the sum of the column totals.

Analyze Two-Way Tables
Relative frequency is how often something happens divided by all outcomes. Frequencies may be displayed as a ratio, a decimal, or a percent. When converting ratios, answers are approximate ($\approx$).

Example: $\frac{50}{51} \approx 0.98$ or 98%

	Passed Test	Failed Test	Totals
Studied for Test	50; $\frac{50}{51} \approx 0.98$	1; $\frac{1}{51} \approx 0.02$	$0.98 + 0.02 \approx 1.00$
Did Not Study for Test	5; $\frac{5}{15} \approx 0.33$	10; $\frac{10}{15} \approx 0.67$	$033 + 0.67 \approx 1.00$
Totals	55; $\frac{55}{66} \approx 0.98$	11; $\frac{11}{66} \approx 0.17$	$0.98 + 0.17 \approx 1.00$

Interpreting Table: Based on the relative frequency value of 0.98 in one of the cells, and the relative frequency value of 0.33 in another cell, you can imply that students who studied were more likely to pass than students who had not.

Finding Relative Frequencies
Step 1: Write the ratios of each value to the total in that row. Divide.
Step 2: Round the answer to the nearest hundredth.
Step 3: Repeat steps 1 and 2 for each column.

Create Your Left-hand Notebook Page
Step 1: Cut out the title and glue it to the top of the notebook page.
Step 2: Complete the table on the *Construct a Two-Way Table* flap book. Cut out the flap book. Cut on the solid line to create two flaps. Apply glue to the back of the top section and attach it below the title. Under each flap, write the definition.
Step 3: Complete the table on the *Relative Frequency* flap book. Cut out the flap book. Cut on the solid line to create two flaps. Apply glue to the back of the top section and attach it at the bottom of the page. Under each flap, write the answer.

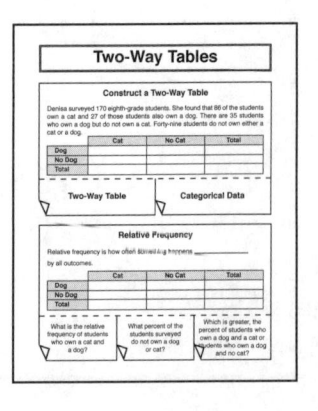

Two-Way Tables

Construct a Two-Way Table

Denisa surveyed 170 eighth-grade students. She found that 86 of the students own a cat and 27 of those students also own a dog. There are 35 students who own a dog but do not own a cat. Forty-nine students do not own either a cat or a dog.

	Cat	No Cat	Total
Dog			
No Dog			
Total			

Two-Way Table

Categorical Data

Relative Frequency

Relative frequency is how often something happens _____ by all outcomes.

	Cat	No Cat	Total
Dog			
No Dog			
Total			

What is the relative frequency of students who own a cat and a dog?

What percent of the students surveyed do not own a dog or cat?

Which is greater, the percent of students who own a dog and a cat or students who own a dog and no cat?

Answer Keys

Answers are limited to those not presented as part of the mini-lessons on each "Student Instructions" page.

Number Systems (p. 5)

Categorizing Real Numbers

Number	Rational Number	Integer	Whole Number	Natural Number
$\frac{2}{6}$	x			
-21	x	x		
0.3	x			
15	x	x	x	x

Converting Repeating Decimals to Fractions (p. 7)
Fraction to Decimal: 0.2, terminating; $0.\overline{27}$, repeating; $0.\overline{4}$, repeating

Repeating Decimal to Fraction: $x = \frac{3}{11}$

Estimating Square Roots (p. 9)
$\sqrt{30} \approx 5.45$ (to the nearest hundredth)

Properties of Integer Exponents (p. 11)
1. Quotient of Powers
2. Zero Power
3. Power of a Product
4. Product of Powers
5. Negative Power
6. Power of a Power

Square Roots & Cube Roots (p. 13)
Perfect Square: 1, 4, 9, 16, 25, 36, 49, 64, 81, 100
Square Root: 1, 2, 3, 4, 5, 6, 7, 8, 9, 10
Perfect Cube: 1, 8, 27, 64, 125, 216, 343, 512, 729, 1,000
Cube Root: 1, 2, 3, 4, 5, 6, 7, 8, 9, 10

Scientific Notation (p. 15)
Standard Form: right, 8 places right, 679,000,000
Scientific Notation: 3.41, 5 places, 3.41×10^5

Adding & Subtracting With Scientific Notation (p. 17)
(clockwise from top) 1.817×10^5; 1.967×10^3; 5.973×10^5; 3.84×10^{-2}

Multiplying & Dividing With Scientific Notation (p. 19)
Multiply: Rule 1, 2.448×10^9; **Divide:** Rule 2, 2.3×10^{-1}

Solving Multi-Step Equations (p. 21)
(clockwise from top) Step 2, Step 4, Step 3, Step 5

Solutions of One-Variable Equations (p. 23)
(clockwise from top) $m = 13$, one solution; $-40 = -40$, infinitely many solutions; $8 = 6$, no solution

Solving Systems of Equations Graphically (p. 25)
Graph 1: Intersecting lines have one point in common; there is one solution to this system.
Graph 2: Parallel lines have no points in common; there is no solution to this system.
Graph 3: Both equations give the same line; there are infinitely many solutions.

Solving Systems of Equations Algebraically (p. 27)
Solve the System: Solution (-3, -4); Solution (1, 6)

Graphing Proportional Relationships (p. 29)
The relationship is proportional.

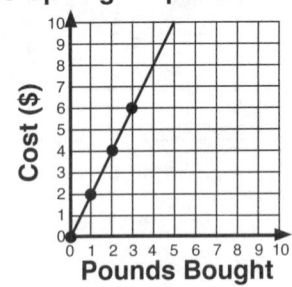

Slope of a Line (p. 31)
Type of Slope: positive; **Slope Ratio:** slope = $\frac{rise}{run}$

y-intercept: (0,4); **Slope:** $\frac{3}{3} = 1$

Similar Triangles and Slope (p. 33)
Corresponding Angles: $\angle U = \angle X$; $\angle V = \angle Y$; $\angle W = \angle Z$

Ratios of Corresponding Sides: $\frac{UV}{XY} = \frac{VW}{YZ} = \frac{WU}{ZX}$

Slope: slope = $\frac{2}{4} = 0.5$

Functions (p. 35)
(Top row left to right) No, the equation has more than one answer for *y*.; Yes, each *y* value has only one corresponding *x* value.; Yes, when you draw a vertical line on the graph, it hits the graphed line in only one spot. (Bottom row left to right) No, when you draw a vertical line on the graph, it hits the graphed line in more than one spot.; Yes, the equation has only one answer for *y*.; No, there is more than one *y* value for some *x* values.

Rate of Change (p. 37)
Graph: Rate of Change

$\frac{y_2 - y_1}{x_2 - x_1}$

$\frac{30 - 10}{3 - 1}$

$\frac{20}{2} = 10$

The rate of change is 10. This means the money earned per hour was $10.

Interactive Math Notebook: Grade 8 — Answer Keys

Table: Rate of Change

$$\frac{y_2 - y_1}{x_2 - x_1}$$
$$\frac{125 - 75}{5 - 3}$$
$$\frac{50}{2} = 25$$

The rate of change is 25. This means $25 worth of tickets were sold each day.

Linear & Nonlinear Functions (p. 39)
Left-Side: (top to bottom) linear, nonlinear, linear, nonlinear
Right-side: (top to bottom) nonlinear, linear, nonlinear, linear

Translations on the Coordinate Plane (p. 41)

Translation Notation $(x, y) \longrightarrow (x + a, y + b)$		
Vertices of △ABC (x, y)	(x + -2, y + 1)	Vertices of △A'B'C' (x, y)
A(-1, -2)	(-1 + -2, -2 + 1)	A'(-3, -1)
B(6, -3)	(6 + -2, -3 + 1)	B'(4, -2)
C(2, -5)	(2 + -2, -5 + 1)	C'(0, -4)

Translation:

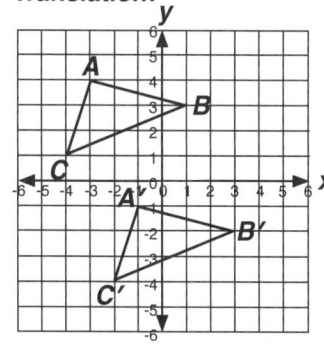

Coordinates:
A'(-1, -1)
B'(3, -2)
C'(-2, -4)

Reflections on the Coordinate Plane (p. 43)
Reflection over x-axis:

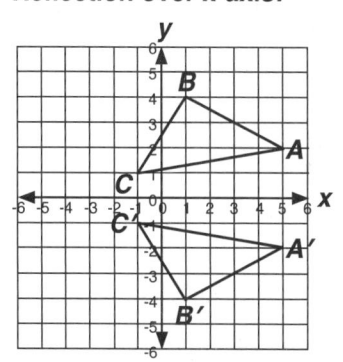

Rule: To reflect a figure over the x-axis, multiply the y-coordinates by -1.
Notation: $(x, y) \rightarrow (x, -y)$
Coordinates: A'(5, -2), B'(1, -4), C'(-1, -1)

Reflection over y-axis:

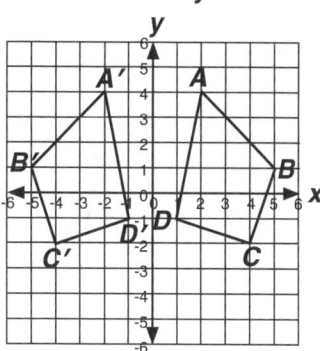

Rule: To reflect a figure over the y-axis, multiply the x-coordinate by -1.
Notation: $(x, y) \rightarrow (-x, y)$
Coordinates: A'(-2, 4), B'(-5, 1), C'(-4, -2), D'(-1, -1)

Rotations on the Coordinate Plane (p. 45)
Triangle ABC:

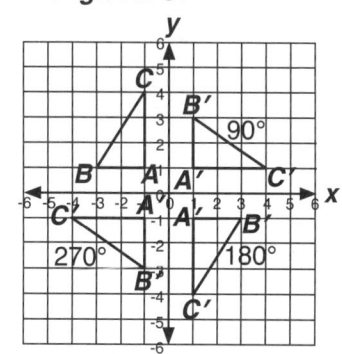

90°: A'(1, 1), B'(1, 3), C'(4, 1)
180°: A'(1, -1), B'(3, -1), C'(1, -4)
270°: A'(-1, -1), B'(-1, -3), C'(-4, -1)

Dilations on the Coordinate Plane (p. 47)
Enlargement:

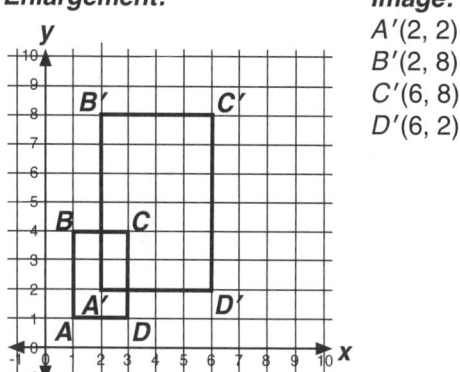

Image:
A'(2, 2)
B'(2, 8)
C'(6, 8)
D'(6, 2)

Reduction:

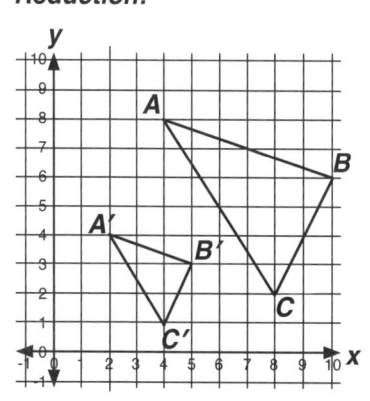

Image:
A'(2, 4)
B'(5, 3)
C'(4, 1)

CD-405047 © Mark Twain Media, Inc., Publishers   61

Answer Keys

Angles of Triangles (p. 49)
Interior Angles: $x = 70°$
Exterior Angles: $x = 150°$

Pythagorean Theorem (p. 51)
Find Missing Length: (left side)
$$a^2 + b^2 = c^2$$
$$3^2 + b^2 = 5^2$$
$$9 - 9 + b^2 = 25 - 9$$
$$b^2 = 16$$
$$b = \sqrt{16}$$
$$b = 4$$
So, the length of side *b* is 4 cm.
Find Missing Length: (right side)
$$a^2 + b^2 = c^2$$
$$6^2 + 8^2 = c^2$$
$$36 + 64 = c^2$$
$$100 = c^2$$
$$\sqrt{100} = c$$
$$10 = c$$
So, the length of side *c* is 10 m.

Distance on a Coordinate Plane (p. 53)

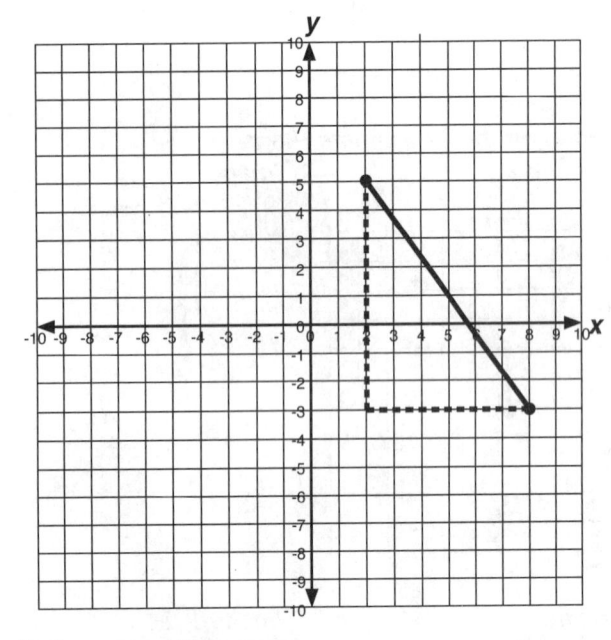

Pythagorean Theorem:
$$a^2 + b^2 = c^2$$
$$6^2 + 8^2 = c^2$$
$$36 + 64 = c^2$$
$$100 = c^2$$
$$\sqrt{100} = c$$
$$10 = c$$
So the distance is 10 units.

Volume of Cones, Cylinders, & Spheres (p. 55)
Cone: Radius of Base = 3 m; Area of Base = 28.26 m^2;
Height = 7 m; Volume = 65.94 m^3
Cylinder: Radius of Base = 4 in.;
Area of Base = 50.24 in.^{2}; Height = 4 in.;
Volume = 200.96 in.^{3}
Sphere: Radius = 2 cm; Value of Radius Cubed = 8 cm;
Pi Times Radius Cubed = 25.12 cm,
Volume = 33.5 cm^3

Scatter Plots (p. 57)
Neighborhood Babysitting Pay:
Association: Positive
Interpret Scatter Plot: As the number of hours worked increased, the amount of money earned increased.
Nesting Female Sea Turtles:
Association: Negative
Interpret Scatter Plot: As the number of years increased, the number of nesting female sea turtles decreased.
Network Reliability:
Association: No oblivious association
Interpret Scatter Plot: The number of connected devices had no obvious effect on the number of network failures.

Two-Way Tables (p. 59)
Construct a Two-Way Table:

	Cat	No Cat	Total
Dog	27	35	62
No Dog	59	49	108
Total	86	84	170

Relative Frequency:

	Cat	No Cat	Total
Dog	27; $\frac{27}{62} \approx 0.44$	35; $\frac{35}{62} \approx 0.56$	$0.44 + 0.56 \approx 1.00$
No Dog	59; $\frac{59}{108} \approx 0.55$	49; $\frac{49}{108} \approx 0.45$	$0.55 + 0.45 \approx 1.00$
Total	86; $\frac{86}{170} \approx 0.51$	84; $\frac{84}{170} \approx 0.49$	$0.51 + 0.49 \approx 1.00$

Cat and dog: $\frac{27}{62} \approx 0.44$ or 44%
No dog or cat: 45%
Greater: Dog and no cat = 56%